THE
LONDON
MAPGUIDE
Michael Middleditch

CONTENTS

Congestion Charge Zone see Page 22

All maps in this Mapguide are based on Aerial Photographs supplied by Aerofilms Ltd.
with an original Ground Survey carried out by MICHAEL GRAHAM Publications.

PENGUIN BOOKS

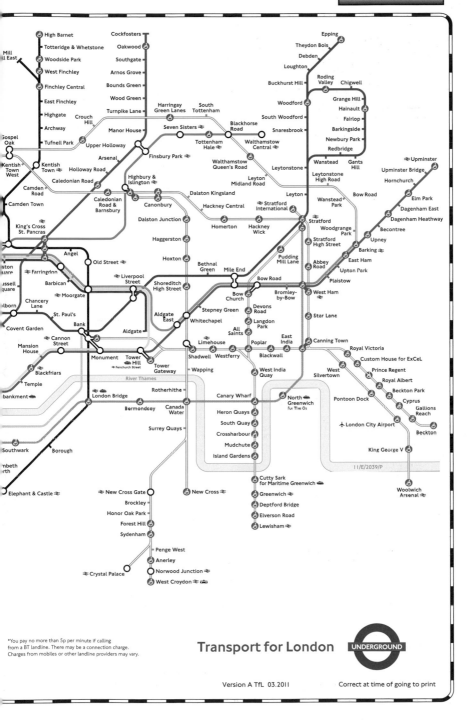

*You pay no more than 5p per minute if calling
from a BT landline. There may be a connection charge.
Charges from mobiles or other landline providers may vary.

Transport for London

UNDERGROUND

Version A TfL 03.2011   Correct at time of going to print

INTRODUCTION AND HISTORY

A RETROSPECT

I was born in London and spent my early life living in a mundane suburb of London, so it was always a great pleasure for me to escape into Central London. My parents must have felt the same for they delighted in walking my brother and me around the city, always stopping at the statues, and grappling with the history relating to the monuments - Edith Cavell (E5 35) was a favourite. At that time London's sky appeared to be full of barrage balloons and there were even sheep in Hyde Park; the avant-garde dance was the *'jitterbug'* imported by American G.I.'s; and the streets seemed to be full of soldiers and sailors from all the countries in the world.

Probably the most exciting day trip was to the London Zoo. This was an annual event and I keenly looked forward to our leisurely planned walk around the confines of what was then a rather cruel way of keeping animals; but it was neverthless exciting. We always went as a family to the theatre at least once a year, the Palladium for variety shows, and then after the war to Drury Lane, the Coliseum and the marvellous Stoll Theatre in Kingsway (long since demolished for an office block), where we saw all the great American musicals.

When I reached my 'teens' it was football and cricket and music as well that attracted me to London. I can't believe how many times I saw opera at Covent Garden in a year - prices have gone up! I remember a concert at the Festival Hall sitting behind the massive shoulders of Vaughan Williams. The 100 Club in Oxford Street (which amazingly is still there) and the bebop clubs scattered around Leicester Square were also popular haunts of mine at that time. Another pastime was roaming and rummaging through Foyles and the numerous secondhand book and record shops in Charing Cross Road looking for bargains. Most of my early working life was spent working in Fleet Street…I loved it - the cosy little pubs scattered around the area offering bitter and home-made food (pre-microwave), and perhaps even a glimpse of my favourite newspaper cartoonist. The office I worked in was on Fleet Street so we were able to see the Lord Mayor's parade and all the visiting dignitaries. I remember rushing out into the street to see my hero Yuri Gagarin - hardly anybody was there to see him, so my friend and I got a special wave. In the evenings I walked back to Liverpool Street Station past bomb damage from the war that had not been reconstructed. In later years my steps were quicker as I eagerly looked forward to seeing my wife and our newborn son in the summer months waiting at the station the other end.

LONDON TODAY

There is no doubt London has changed: a certain continental air pervades, people sit on pavements in inclement weather sipping coffee. Covent Garden piazza has thankfuly been preserved - no vegetables but a lively shopping and eating area; Camden Lock is now a young people's preserve with a large market; Soho is no longer full of strip clubs - you are more likely to see men kissing and cuddling in public! The old financial area has been re-invented with a number of interesting and controversial buildings, and a few eyesores; Ludgate railway bridge no longer obscures the view of St. Paul's, though the city area is still as big a hodge-podge as it was in Wren's day! Young people who were born in the suburbs seem now to prefer to live in Central London again, I can understand that…that's life!

THE STREETS OF LONDON

London was no more than a swamp (*Llyn-dyn* in Celtic means a stronghold by the marsh) when the Romans first pitched camp on the northside of the Thames in AD 43, and built their town: it was called *Londinium* and was located between the Tower as it is now, and where the River Fleet used to enter the Thames close by the present Blackfriars Bridge. They built the first wooden bridge across the Thames (at the bisection of the town area) and a stone wall which, if it had been built a century earlier, might have stopped the warrior queen Boudicca from burning the town. Londinium was the heart of the Roman province of *Britannia* and the capital; it had a very large prestigious basilica (a Roman law court building) and forum (market place) which would encompass Gracechurch Street. Like so much of London, the street names tell the story: 'Walbrook' was once a small stream which ran through the centre of the Roman town.

When the legions finally withdrew in AD 410 after the collapse of the Roman Empire, civilization declined; the Walbrook flooded again and the town fell into ruins. For an idea of how London looked then visit the Museum of London (D2 36).

Overrun by Angles, Saxons and Jutes, the British fled westwards to Wales leaving what then became known as *Angleland* (England) to the marauders. Although the invaders were heathens it did not take long before Christianity had gained a footing and churches began to appear: St.Paul's was founded in the year 604 and a monastery was established at Westminster. London's importance only began to recover during the reign (871-901) of King Alfred the Great: he made London habitable again. Alfred built a navy which tussled with

and beat the Danish and Norse pirates who were rampaging continuously up the creeks and rivers. Eventually when peace came the Danes were allowed to settle and Canute became the King - he was also King of Denmark. The Strand (F5 35) - then a suburb of London - and Southwark on the other side of the Thames were Danish enclaves.

FRENCH CONNECTION

Having spent a great deal of his early life in Normandy, Edward the Confessor was enamoured with the Norman style of building, which was an extension of the Romanesque. He established the early palace and abbey at Westminster, where he was crowned. He died in 1066 and the Norsemen or Normans who had adopted the French language arrived and William the Conqueror became King. He built the Tower of London - the White Tower - (see page 53) which still stands today. Probably one of the finest examples of the Norman-style of church building to be seen in the city is the church of St.Bartholomew the Great (C2 36). The French contribution to architecture and in particular to the building of cathedrals with stone roofs gradually culminated in the pointed Gothic style, and with the establishment of English-Gothic architecture.

Today it is difficult to imagine that the Houses of Parliament stand on what was once the small island of Thorney - the site of the early Westminster Abbey which was demolished by King Henry III in 1205, when centuries of construction commenced on the building of the Abbey (E4 43) as we see it now.

MEDIEVAL TIMES

London had become three districts during this period: the City, Westminster and Southwark - which was connected to the

EDITH CAVELL MEMORIAL (E5 35)
'PATRIOTISM IS NOT ENOUGH I MUST HAVE NO HATRED OR BITTERNESS FOR ANYONE'

OLD LONDON BRIDGE BY CLAUDE DE JONGH

city by the old stone London Bridge, which lasted from 1209-1756, and had houses and even a chapel built on top of it. Southwark was renowned for brothels and other entertainments: bull and bear rings were attractions long before Shakespeare's 'Globe' arrived in 1599, and it has returned again, thanks to the years of endeavour by the American actor Sam Wanamaker who finally managed to get the theatre reconstructed close to the original site (D6 36).

Westminster housed the royal residence until it finally became the home of Parliament during Henry VIII's reign. Westminster Hall is all that is left to see of this original building if you do visit the Houses of Parliament. In the City the merchants established their guilds and they elected the first mayor of London in 1188; the City has remained autonomous since that time. There were also large priories at Blackfriars and Whitefriars - friars unlike monks were in the beginning working Christians who tended the sick and needy; in *The Canterbury Tales* Chaucer gives another view. Henry VIII banned monks and friars and unfortunately he knocked down many beautiful abbeys and monasteries.

GROWTH - FIRE - PROSPERITY

Towards the end of the Tudor lineage London's population had reached almost 200,000. Henry VIII had laid out Hyde Park and St. James's Park and moved the royal palace to Whitehall, but it was his daughter Elizabeth I who was probably responsible for the growth of the city: she granted the East India Company the monopoly of trade with the eastern hemisphere. This was the beginning of London as a financial centre. After abolishing the monarchy and to a certain degree self-inflicting Oliver Cromwell on themselves, the British people returned to monarchy with restrictions. After centuries of exclusion, Cromwell had allowed Jews to settle in London, and this was certainly good for finances and the country.

In 1666 after a terrible plague, fire broke out destroying most of the city and the old St. Paul's. The phoenix was Christopher Wren (see page 14), whose plan for the city was never allowed to come to fruition as people hastened to rebuild without a great deal of attention to planning. The Monument (G5 37) was designed by Wren and was erected near where the fire started; who could ever dispute the uplift that St Paul's gives to the spirits of Londoners? When the 18th century dawned the Bank of England had been founded for just six years and London had become the largest financial centre in the world, overtaking Amsterdam. Residential districts grew in Lincoln's Inn and Covent Garden, which already had the marvellous Inigo Jones piazza and St. Paul's church. London's famous landmark squares were also laid out as the century proceeded. The trade with the east brought the phenomenon of coffee houses, where business was often transacted.

In 1811 the country had a Prince Regent (later George IV) and a certain architectural style which is attributed to the architect John Nash who was reponsible for one of London's joys - the lovely Cumberland Terrace (H3 25) that overlooks Regent's Park. The Haymarket Theatre (D6 34) and also a considerable part of Buckingham Palace (A3 42) are attributed to him.

DICKENS' LONDON

London during Queen Victoria's reign was the capital of a huge and much envied empire, and the scene of a great deal of squalor - not a cardboard city then and certainly not as jolly as a Christmas card, but without doubt the inspiration for the art and heart of Charles Dickens. Many of his locations are still very much the same as they were in his day, particularly around the Temple area (H4 35). The River Thames was spanned by most of the bridges we see today and with the advent of the steam engine, railways were constructed enabling London to spread even further afield. The villages of Islington, Hampstead and Highgate were no longer separate, yet strangely if you visit them, a certain amount of village atmosphere still prevails. The central station terminuses were built - St. Pancras (E3 27) is a monument itself to the steam age and is Londons finest station.

Another man who never forgot his roots in Lambeth (A5 44) was Charlie Chaplin whose autobiography vividly describes his life in south London at the end of the 19th century, when music halls and pubs became escapes from the tedium of work. Although many theatres have disappeared there are plenty of pubs to get the feel of life in those days.

MILLENNIUM

By the beginning of the 20th century London's population had reached 6.5 million, larger than Paris and New York. It had spread far and wide due to the underground system that enabled commuters to travel quickly into central London. Unscathed by the Great War, much of the city was destroyed later when the Second World War started. Hitler attempted to demoralize the British people with his 'blitzkreig', which like a tinderbox set London's East End and docks on fire: the red skies of those autumn nights of 1940 are indelible on my memory.

Although reconstruction was slow after the war, the Festival of Britain in 1951 did inaugurate new forms of building and architecture - the Festival Hall (G1 43) is an example of this period. Today within the labyrinth of the city you will discover the amazing and interesting diversity of the architecture - although you cannot always see some features due to the closeness of the building - that is the unique character of the City of London. However in Canary Wharf (64) and Paddington Basin (A2 32) the best of London's 21st century integrated urban planning shines through.

Try the canal-side walk from the Zoo or Camden market to Little Venice and then on to the Basin where you can take a rest in a restaurant or café and watch the world go by. For a good view over London's roof-tops, walk up Primrose Hill (E1 25). A plaque at the top explains the panorama for you.

ARCHITECTURE AND PLANNING

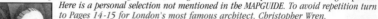

LONDON'S ARCHITECTURE AND ARCHITECTS A great deal of Central London was built in the 19th century; this was also when one of the features of London - its lovely squares and crescents - were built; many of these are situated in Paddington (30-33), Kensington (38-40), and Belgravia (41). Islington too has some squares from the Georgian period.

Here is a personal selection not mentioned in the MAPGUIDE. To avoid repetition turn to Pages 14-15 for London's most famous architect, Christopher Wren.

ENGLISH PALLADIANISM

INIGO JONES (1573-1652) On journeying to Italy around 1600 he was influenced by the style of the architect Andrea Palladio; later, when he became Surveyor General (preceding Wren), he built in white Portland stone the Banqueting House (see Page 11). His plan for Covent Garden Piazza (F4 35) was possibly London's first true open square. On the west side stands St Paul's, the actors' church - in Jones's early life he was associated with theatrical design, often with Ben Jonson. The church is entered

COVENT GARDEN PIAZZA

through the churchyard and was featured in the film *My Fair Lady*. In 1795 the inside church was gutted by fire: when it was restored the side galleries were not replaced.

ENGLISH BAROQUE

NICHOLAS HAWKSMOOR (1661-1736) At the age of 18 he started working for Christopher Wren, and with him he was part of the Baroque movement: his work although in the shadow of Wren is extremely original and has been often undervalued. Near the British Museum is one of the most unusual of his six London churches - St George's (E2 35).The top of the tower is crowned with a stepped pyramid steeple surmounted by a statue of King George 1. Crawling up the pyramid on the corners are two lions and two unicorns both ten-foot high!

ST GEORGE'S

REGENCY LONDON

Although a millwright's son, **JOHN NASH (1752-1835)**, at the age of 61, after a chequered start in London, became the Prince Regent's favourite architect. Renowned for his visionary town planning, he designed the royal route, starting from the Prince Regent's house in Carlton House Terrace (overlooking St James's Park) northwards to Regent's Park: on the way he created Waterloo Place, the Theatre Royal Haymarket, the former Regent Circus now Piccadilly Circus, and at Langham Place he built his only church, All Souls (A2 34). His landscaping scheme for Regent's Park, encompassing it with a wonderful array of terraces, is superb. My favourite overlooking the park is the majestic Cumberland Terrace (H3 25) with its lovely portico and Wedgwood blue painted stucco. At the same time as he was building the mughul-inspired Royal Pavilion in Brighton in 1823, he built Sussex Place (D5 24) on the park's west side. Nash's building with its octagonal domes almost

ALL SOULS (A2 34)

complements the nearby mosque which was built in 1978. Many of his buildings today have been demolished or rebuilt keeping their façades with modernised living areas. In Regent Street, architectural unity is still retained in spite of the early 1900's Beaux Arts redevelopment to accommodate larger stores and shops.

VICTORIAN TIMES

The early 1800's saw the emergence of railways culminating in the great stations which appeared along what was the New Road, whic h today is Marylebone, Euston and Pentonville Roads. The extending city, built without an overall plan, had by the mid 19th century to deal with sewage problems, and roads to transport people to the ring of new stations.

SIR GEORGE GILBERT SCOTT (1811-1878) was one of the leading architects responsible for the Gothic revival in England. The frontage of St Pancras Station 1866-68 with the former Midland Hotel is one of his finest achievements: it is a most colourful building, recently given a clean-up to take the soot off to reveal the red brick and grey and beige stonework. Nearly demolished in the 1960s, it was saved by the efforts of the Poet Laureate Sir John Betjeman whose statue stands in the arcade concourse gazing at the Barlow Shed roof, which has a single-span of 76m - the widest enclosed space in the world for many years.

ST PANCRAS STATION (E3 27)

UNDERGROUND

In 1863 the first underground railway the **METROPOLITAN LINE** gouged its way from Paddington to Farringdon along the New Road. Not a tunnel but 'cut and cover', it took three years to construct and was a great success. This tube line is still the most comfortable for me, it is less claustrophobic - the trains are higher and wider than the other lines.

SIR JOSEPH BAZALGETTE (1819-1891) was responsible for cleaning up London: his plan for sewage tunnels eradicated cholera, and due to his foresight the pipe and tunnel gauges were built to handle the population expansion. He was the architect of the Albert and Chelsea Embankments, and the wonderful Victoria Embankment (F6 35): the

CUT AND COVER

wall reclaiming the foreshore of the river which is a lovely walk from Big Ben to Blackfriars Bridge. Underneath lies a huge sewage tunnel which runs on to Beckton in east London. With Charles Henry Driver he designed the exotic *Cathedral of Sewage* Abbey Mills Pumping Station (G6 61), a very unusual building in a Gothic Byzantine style with a dome like an Eastern Orthodox church. The building has been used in several films including *Batman Begins*.

ABBEY MILLS PUMPING STATION

TWENTY / TWENTY-FIRST CENTURIES

During the first few decades of the twentieth century the electrified extension to the underground system and cheaper housing in the outer suburbs brought the inhabitants of METROLAND into the expanding city.

HAMPSTEAD GARDEN SUBURB (B 56)

In 1904 SIR RAYMOND UNWIN (1863 - 1940) was responsible for planning the world's first garden city - Letchworth in Hertfordshire. Four years later he was asked by a social reformer and idealist Henrietta Barnett (1851-1936) to plan a model community to house mixed social classes in an area of 650 acres backing onto Hampstead Heath: the idea was that the rich would help the poorer tenants. Canon Barnett, her husband, had preached for many years to the poor in London's East End, and both were practical socialists. The suburb to this day is more or less a haven for the liberal middle class. Among the former residents are: the actor Robert Donat (Mr Chips) 8 Meadway, Prime Minister Harold Wilson 10-12 Southway, and surprisingly Elizabeth Taylor who lived at 8 Wildwood Road. The Central Square is truly a sight to see; it has two facing churches, both designed by SIR EDWIN LUTYENS (1869-1944), the architect who designed the Cenotaph (E2 43) in Whitehall, and was well known for his later work in New Delhi. One of the churches is St Jude, the name of the church where Canon Barnett (Henrietta's husband) preached in London's East End. Lutyens also designed the highly regarded Institute situated on the east side of the square.

ST JUDE ON CENTRAL SQUARE

SEE PAGE 56

OLD DAILY EXPRESS

MODERN MOVEMENT   I worked for fifteen years in Fleet Street and the two press buildings that stood out, and still do, are the *Daily Telegraph* and the *Daily Express* - which was my favourite. Both newspapers are no longer situated there, leaving no major Industry in the city centre. The *Express* was built in 1932 by SIR OWEN WILLIAMS (1890-1969) who was a structural engineer and architect with a skill for concrete construction: he was responsible for much of the 1923 British Empire exhibition. Later Williams worked on the structure of the *Daily Telegraph*: his finest architectural achievement is the art-deco *Daily Express* building (B3 36) with its exterior of vitrolite (black pigmented glass) and clear glass, which could claim to be one of the first truly modern buildings in the city. The lobby has some wonderful art-deco bronze reliefs by *Eric Aumonier*. The present occupants are the international investment bankers Goldman Sachs.

THE THAMES FLOOD BARRIER

In 1953 a surge of tide in the River Thames killed over 300 people. This tragedy initiated the construction of a barrier close to Woolwich (see map Page 64). The barrier is 518 metres wide with ten steel clad gates, which when closing rotate 90°, reaching a height of 18 metres.

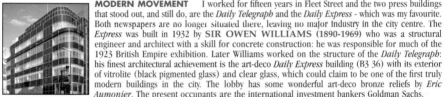

THAMES FLOOD BARRIER

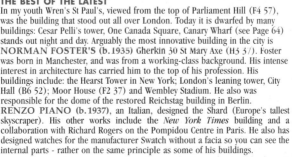

CHARING CROSS STATION

CHARING CROSS STATION

In 1990 the station (E6 35) behind the Victorian hotel was covered by offices and a shopping centre called Embankment Place. It was designed by SIR TERRY FARRELL (b.1938). More of his interesting work can be seen at Paddington Basin (B2 32), and further down the Thames where he built the new MI6 Headquarters (F2 51).

THE ROLLING BRIDGE

At Paddington Basin across the canal there is a very unusual small foot bridge (B2 32) conceived by THOMAS HEATHERWICK (b.1970), the man who designed the 2012 Olympic Cauldron and the new bus for London which has now been given the nickname *Boris Bus*! The bridge rolls up into an octagon to allow barges through. A unique design, it is the only one in the world at this time. Every Friday at midday you can view the bridge curling up to allow for maintenance.

THE BEST OF THE LATEST

In my youth Wren's St Paul's, viewed from the top of Parliament Hill (F4 57), was the building that stood out all over London. Today it is dwarfed by many buildings: Cesar Pelli's tower, One Canada Square, Canary Wharf (see Page 64) stands out night and day. Arguably the most innovative building in the city is NORMAN FOSTER'S (b.1935) Gherkin 30 St Mary Axe (H3 37). Foster was born in Manchester, and was from a working-class background. His intense interest in architecture has carried him to the top of his profession. His buildings include: the Hearst Tower in New York; London's leaning tower, City Hall (B6 52); Moor House (F2 37) and Wembley Stadium. He also was responsible for the dome of the restored Reichstag building in Berlin.

RENZO PIANO (b.1937), an Italian, designed the Shard (Europe's tallest skyscraper). His other works include the *New York Times* building and a collaboration with Richard Rogers on the Pompidou Centre in Paris. He also has designed watches for the manufacturer Swatch without a facia so you can see the internal parts - rather on the same principle as some of his buildings.

THE GHERKIN

THE SHARD

THE BRITISH MUSEUM

Map reference E2 35 Set in Bloomsbury this is truly a great museum - in the top league with few rivals - and it is the most popular museum in London. This superb building houses an immense collection of treasures from all over the world. It was built in 1852 in the neo-classical style by the architect Robert Smirke, and if you approach the museum from the south, you view a magnificent Ionic-colonnaded façade with a pediment containing allegorical sculptures that represent the progress of the human race in Art and Science etc. The museum was founded in 1753, when physician Sir Hans Sloane's library and varied collection of over 80,000 objects, including plants, fossils, coins and manuscripts, was purchased by the government with proceeds of a public lottery. The first home of the museum was on the present site in a 17th century mansion known as Montague House, which disappeared when the existing building was constructed. The azure, round 'Reading Room' which is absolutely magnificent was finished in 1857 and is the work of Smirke's younger brother Sydney. In the centre of the area - originally an open quadrangle - Smirke built his dome which is over 140 feet in diameter, and is wider than the dome of St. Peter's in Rome. With the removal of the 'British Library' to St.Pancras and the beginning of the new century, a glass roof was constructed to span the two acre courtyard and dome; it has been renamed the 'Great Court'.

THE MARVELS OF ATHENS

There is no doubt that the 'Elgin Marbles', are one of the museums greatest attractions, and it is very easy to understand why the Greeks would like to see them returned to Athens. Collected by the Earl of Elgin in 1801, they were sold to the British government in 1816. Originally these sculptures, reckoned by many people to be the greatest classical carvings in the world, adorned the 438 BC Parthenon - the Temple of Athene Parthenos (the virgin) - which overlooks Athens from the Acropolis hill. It is quite likely they would have been broken up if Elgin had not acquired them - who knows? You can view these wonders on the ground floor in the Duveen Gallery, which was purpose built in 1938 to exhibit them.

MADNESS IN GREAT ONES

Staring eyes have always seemed to me to be linked with some form of madness: I think of Hitler, Mosley and other such gangsters. The bust of the Roman emperor Augustus (27BC - AD14) is striking for his piercing eyes inlaid with marble and glass, and his posture. He was not mad though: related to Julius Caeser, he became Rome's first Emperor and set about undoing military dictatorship and making the empire more constitutional. See room 70.

METALLIC BEAUTY

In the centre of room 33 is the 8th century figure of Tara a goddess from Sri Lanka in gilded bronze. The sculpting of material is sheer beauty.

THE MUMMIES OF EGYPT

Children always seem to have a strange fascination for the bandaged mummies inside their exotic cases, and there are rooms full of them to contemplate. I was frightened as a small child (pre-Hammer) when I was taken to the cinema, so I would not be the night watchman in this gallery. Here too, is 'Ginger', a man born over 5000 years ago, who was near so perfectly preserved in hot desert sand - he was given his name because of the colour of his hair.

SUTTON HOO TREASURE

In 1939 the remains of a 7th century ship were accidently found in a Suffolk field. The ship contained the treasures of an Anglo-Saxon king, who had been buried with his worldly acquisitions, including many interesting pieces of jewellery in gold and enamel which are well preserved and worth seeking out. His helmet is really stunning and although once fragmented it has been very carefully restored.

REFLECTION

With such a vast selection you have to make your own choice. Here are a few that might interest you: an amazing 1585 ship clock (the dial is at the foot of the main mast) made in Prague, elegant Chinese porcelain, the Roman 'Lycurgus Cup' in green glass that changes ruby-red in light and with wine, Isle of Lewis 12th century chessmen, Venetian glass, amazing collections of coins, and the 'Rosetta Stone'. Drawings by Dürer, Michelangelo, Watteau, Claude Lorrain, and Turner are not necessarily on display but they can be viewed.

The Museum shop is an ideal place to buy presents or souvenirs to remind you of your visit to London. Prints, scarves, books, jewellery, and replicas of many of the museums sculptures are on sale.

Once inside the museum obtain a museum floor plan; you will need it!

GROUND FLOOR

GREEK & ROMAN
Including Bassae sculpture, the Nereid Monument - Sculptures from the Parthenon.
WESTERN ASIA
Ancient Palestine - Assyrian sculpture - Khorsabad, Nimrud, and Nineveh palace reliefs.
EGYPTIAN SCULPTURE
ORIENTAL COLLECTIONS
China, South and Southeast Asia - Amaravati sculpture - Islamic art.
ETHNOGRAPHY
The Mexican Gallery
THE READING ROOM

BASEMENT

GREEK and ROMAN
Architecture - Greek Sculpture - Ephesus
WESTERN ASIA
Ishtar Temple - Assyrian art.

UPPER FLOORS

PREHISTORIC & ROMANO-BRITISH
Stone Age (mezzanine) - Prehistory - Roman Britain
MEDIEVAL, RENAISSANCE and MODERN
Medieval tiles and pottery - clocks & watches - Waddesdon Bequest -
Europe 15th, 18th, 19th centuries -
Europe & America 20th century.
WESTERN ASIA Ancient Iran, Anatolia - Syria - Nimrud ivories - South Arabia
EGYPT Mummies - Tomb paintings and Papyri - Egypt and Africa - Coptic Egypt.
COINS and MEDALS
GREEK and ROMAN
Rome: City & Empire -
Pre-Roman Empire Italy-
Ancient Cyprus -
Greeks in Southern Italy.
PRINTS & DRAWINGS
ORIENTAL COLLECTIONS
Japanese Galleries.

Monday-Thursday, Saturday, Sunday 10.00-17.00, Friday 10.00-20.30   *Free*

MUSEUMS AND ART GALLERIES

APSLEY HOUSE, WELLINGTON MUSEUM G2 41

149 Piccadilly, W1. Built in 1778 by the Adam brothers: the Duke purchased the house from his brother after his famous victory at Waterloo. Until his death in 1852, a banquet was held in the house to commemorate his finest hour. Filled with pictures, porcelain, silver, plate and other relics of the Iron Duke. Probably the most singularly interesting item is the larger than life nude statue of his adversary Napoleon: one room of the house is decorated like a military tent of that era.
Tuesday - Sunday 11.00 - 17.00. *Charge*

BANK OF ENGLAND MUSEUM F3 37
Bartholomew Lane, EC2. Chronicling monetary history this museum resides within the walls of the great city bank. Models, bank notes, gold bars the complexities of exchanging money and dealing on the foreign exchanges will interest budding traders.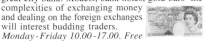
Monday-Friday 10.00-17.00. Free

CHARLES DICKENS MUSEUM* G6 27
48 Doughty Street, WC1. From 1837-39, Dickens lived in this four-floored terraced house and wrote his novels *Oliver Twist* and *Nicholas Nickleby* during that period. His manuscripts, photographs, and lantern slides etc. are on view.
Daily 10.00 - 17.00. *Charge*

CLOCKMAKERS' MUSEUM E3 37
Guildhall, Aldermanbury, EC2. Attached to the Guildhall is this small museum. Watches, clocks and the chronometers used at sea to establish the position of longitude are here: includes John Harrison's H5.
Monday - Saturday 9.30 - 16.45. *Free*

COURTAULD GALLERY G5 35
Somerset House, Strand, WC2. This is a superb collection of Impressionist and Post-Impressionist paintings and many other works bequeathed to the University of London. The finest of its kind in Britain, the collection includes works by Renoir, Degas, Manet, Monet, Seurat, Gauguin and Van Gogh, as well as Rubens and Van Dyck. *Charge Daily 10.00-18.00 Free for under 18s, Mondays are Free 10.00 - 14.00 except Bank Holidays.*

DESIGN MUSEUM D6 52
Shad Thames, SE1 2YD. A rather austere building dedicated to 20-21st century design and focusing on everyday mass produced objects from motorbikes to household gadgets. *Daily 10.00 - 17.45. Charge*

GUARDS MUSEUM C3 42
Wellington Barracks, Birdcage Walk, SW1. The Guards regiments were founded in the 17th century and their history is recalled with their weapons, uniforms, trophies and personal belongings.
Daily 10.00 - 16.00. *Charge*

HANDEL HOUSE MUSEUM H4 33

25 Brook Street, W1 Music and the interior decorations recreate the time from 1723-59 when the Royal Fireworks composer Georg Friedrich Händel once lived, worked and died in this house. *Tues, Weds, Fris, Sats, 10.00-18.00, Thurs 20.00 Suns 12.00-18.00 Charge*

HAYWARD GALLERY G1 43
South Bank, SE1. Adjoining the Queen Elizabeth Hall, the gallery is used for major art exhibitions. Always interesting displays, which is more than you can say for the exterior of the building.
Daily 10.00 - 18.00, Thurs & Fris 20.00 Charge

IMPERIAL WAR MUSEUM A5 44

Lambeth Road, SE1. Once part of a lunatic asylum called 'Bedlam', the museum illustrates the history of the two world wars and also more recent combat operations that involved Britain. You can experience what it was like in the trenches and in the East End of London during the Blitz. Large collections of photographs, paintings, decorations, weapons, uniforms, and full size aircraft suspended from the ceiling. *Daily 10.00-18.00 Free*

JEWISH MUSEUM H1 25
129-131 Albert Street, N1. Situated in Camden in a stylish extended townhouse you will find a collection of Jewish antiquities that illustrate both the private and the public religious life and history of the Jewish community in Britain. *Sunday-Thurs 10.00-17.00. Fris 14.00 Closed Bank & Jewish Holidays. Charge*

LEIGHTON HOUSE C4 38
12 Holland Park Road, Kensington W14. Home of the celebrated Victorian artist Lord Leighton, who lived here until his death in 1896. Permanently on display are examples of High Victorian art with works by Leighton, Burne-Jones and Millais. The house is renowned for the beautiful Arab Hall, an authentic reconstruction of a Moorish palace banqueting hall. Fine period rooms of Victorian furniture, a collection of William de Morgan pottery and an attractive garden. Evening concerts.
Wednesday - Monday 10.00 - 17.30. *Charge*

LONDON CANAL MUSEUM F2 27
12-13 New Wharf Road, N1 9RT. The story of the canals and the people who lived on the narrow boats.
Tuesday - Sunday 10.00 - 16.30. *Charge*

LONDON TRANSPORT MUSEUM F4 35
Covent Garden WC2. In the flower market building of Covent Garden. This interesting museum illustrates the development of London's transport system with historic buses, trams, trolleybuses, and rail vehicles. *Daily 10.00 - 18.30, opens 11.00 on Fridays* *Charge*

MUSEUM OF LONDON D2 36

Barbican, London Wall, EC2. An intriguing display that defines the history, topography and rich heritage of London from prehistoric times to the present day. Roman remains, models of the Roman forum and baths, Anglo-Saxon material, furniture and clothing from Tudor and Stuart times, reconstructed shops and offices of Victorian and Edwardian days are just a few of the imaginative displays to be seen. Always attracting attention is the magnificent Lord Mayor's golden state coach and the Art-Deco elevator which used to whisk you to the restaurant at Selfridges. Look closely at the Map of Poverty on the walls and ceiling of a small alcove.
Daily 10.00 - 18.00 Open Bank Holidays *Free*

NATIONAL ARMY MUSEUM E3 49
Royal Hospital Rd, Chelsea, SW3. Imaginatively recording the story of British, Indian, and colonial land forces from Tudor times to the present day. Uniforms, weapons and personal relics of some great military leaders. Over 62,000 French, Prussian and English soldiers were killed at Waterloo in 1815. You can see a model of the battle and a film of it.
Daily 10.00 - 17.30 *Free*

NATIONAL GALLERY   D6 34

Trafalgar Square, WC2. Situated in the domain of London's pigeons, the gallery holds an unequalled collection representing the European schools of painting and it is particularly rich in examples of Dutch and Italian works. There is also a large selection of British paintings from the works of Hogarth to Turner. Modern paintings are not on display here, for the cut-off year is 1900. Colourful works like Van Gogh's *Sunflowers*, the last Turner paintings and his *Fighting Temeraire*, Renoir's *Umbrellas*, and Seurat's *Bathers at Asnières* are all here. There are also some marvellous dreamy Claude Lorrain canvases, the classic *Haywain* by Constable and the *Rokeby Venus* by Velázquez.
Daily 10.00 - 18.00, Friday 21.00,   *Free*

NATIONAL PORTRAIT GALLERY   D5 34

St. Martin's Place, WC2. Interesting and often topical, this gallery tucked into the side of the National Gallery always holds your attention. Shakespeare to the Rolling Stones, that is the variety you get. Here are a few: all the Kings and Queens, John Donne, Cromwell, Nell Gwyn, the Brönte sisters, Lily Langtry, Byron, and Bernard Shaw. A couple of my favourites are Noel Coward, and the great Manchester United footballer Bobby Charlton
Daily 10.00-18.00, Thurs and Fris 10.00-21.00. Free

NATURAL HISTORY MUSEUM   A5 40

Cromwell Rd. South Kensington, SW7. Built in 1880 in the romanesque style, this fine, colourful terracotta building has zoological decorations along its wide facade. The departments incorporate Botany, Entomology, Minerology, Paleontology, Zoology and the Museum of Geology, renamed the 'Earth Galleries', and has some interesting features - an escalator ride through a portion of a rotating globe to the 'Power Within' exhibition which explains volcanos and simulates an earthquake. The film *Jurassic Park* stimulated interest in dinosaurs, and this museum has a moving, roaring, virtually real, almost frightening dinosaur! The new **Darwin Centre** building is a must-see expansion to the museum.....state-of-the-art science!
Daily 10.00 - 17.50.   *Free*

QUEEN'S GALLERY, THE   A3 42

Buckingham Palace Rd. SW1. Formerly the private chapel of Buckingham Palace, now used as an exhibition gallery, changing annually to display to the public a small part of the vast royal collection which includes famous artists' works, drawings, photographs and other works of art.   *Charge*
Open during exhibitions 10.00 - 17.30
Entrance by Timed Tickets   ☎ 020 7766 7301

ROYAL ACADEMY OF ARTS   B6 34

Burlington House, Piccadilly, W1. Founded in 1768 by Joshua Reynolds whose statue stands in the courtyard, the Academy is famous for its annual Summer Exhibition from May to September, which exhibits the works of living artists. Other exhibitions are also held throughout the year.
Daily 10.00 - 18.00, Fridays 22.00   *Charge*

SCIENCE MUSEUM   B4 40

Exhibition Rd. SW7. I always enjoyed my trips as a child to this museum; it was one of the first to allow you to interact in the discovery process. I have no doubt that children today find this museum one of the most interesting to visit. The museum traces many of the great achievements in the history and development of science and industry, and displays on five floors some of the original machines and equipment: steam engines like Stephenson's *Rocket* along with modern prototype locomotives. Mitchell's famous *Schneider Trophy Seaplane*, the forerunner of the Spitfire; the *Apollo 10* command module; veteran cars, and many other experiences that you can participate in: you can fly a plane, be an air traffic controller, mix and record music etc. IMAX cinema book on ☎ *0870 870 4771   Charge Museum opens daily 10.00 - 18.00,   Free*

SIR JOHN SOANE'S MUSEUM   G3 35

13 Lincoln's Inn Fields, WC2. Son of a bricklayer Sir John Soane (1753-1837) was an architect who was responsible for the windowless (for security) exterior wall of the Bank of England. His art collection and atmospheric house is filled like a magician's box with unforeseen revelations: Hogarth, Canaletto, Watteau, Reynolds, Turner and others are here along with Egyptian and Roman antiquities.
First Tuesday of the month 18.00 - 21.00,
Tuesday - Saturday 10.00 - 17.00.   *Free*

TATE BRITAIN   E1 51

Millbank, SW1. Facing the Thames, this gallery contains British art from Tudor times onwards; the Turner collection is magnificent and includes his cerulean Venice paintings. You can view Hogarth, Constable, William Blake, the Pre-Raphaelites, Walter Sickert, etc., and sculptures by Henry Moore and Jacob Epstein. The restaurant is also notable, but it is unfortunately not open in the evenings.
Open Daily 10.00 - 18.00, Friday 22.00   Free

TATE MODERN   C6 36

Bankside, SE1. Opened in 2000, the original Turbine Hall of the renovated Bankside power station makes an impressive introduction to this eclectic collection of international arts of the 20-21st centuries, includes works by Francis Bacon, Cézanne, Bonnard, Dali, Roy Lichtenstein, Magritte, Matisse, Mirò, Picasso etc., and sculptures by Rodin and Constantin Brancusi. On the top floor is a café which has fine views across London.   *Suns - Thurs 10.00 - 18.00, Fris - Sats 10.00 - 22.00.*   *Free*

VICTORIA AND ALBERT MUSEUM   B5 40

Cromwell Rd, South Kensington, SW7. One of the world's great and inspirational art collections with displays of fine and applied art of all countries, periods and styles. There are the great cartoons (tapestry patterns) executed by Raphael in 1516 for Pope Leo X, a large number of works by Constable, Tiffany glass, Limoges enamels, Post-Classical sculpture, Indian art, a Frank Lloyd Wright gallery, and at the rear of the museum the Morris and Gamble rooms, which are also worth seeking out. They used to be restaurant rooms.
Daily 10.00 - 17.45, Friday 22.00   *Free*

WALLACE COLLECTION   F3 33

Manchester Sq. W1. A superb collection of art from all periods and from many lands especially France: pictures- Watteau's *La Toilette* - and 17th-18th century porcelain and furniture. There are also many examples of European and Oriental arms and armour, terracotta, jewellery, bronzes, and pictures by Flemish, Spanish and Italian masters. *The Laughing Cavalier* by Hals - the man that made lace come alive on canvas - is here!
Daily 10.00 - 17.00   *Free*
Sir Richard Wallace donated over 100 drinking fountains to the city of Paris

PLACES OF INTEREST

ALBERT MEMORIAL A3 40
Kensington Gore, SW7. This memorial was not of Albert's wish; nevertheless it is very impressive and is, if anything, a memorial to Victorian arts and crafts. The Prince Consort (1819-61) sits under a canopy holding the catalogue to the Great Exhibition of 1851, beneath him is a high relief frieze of 200 figures: musicians, poets, painters etc.

BANQUETING HOUSE E2 43
Whitehall, SW1. The only part of Whitehall Palace to survive the Great Fire. Designed in the Palladian style and built with Portland stone by Inigo Jones, it dates from 1619 and is noted for the fine allegorical ceiling paintings by Rubens. Occasionally closed for government functions and concerts. Check ☎ 3166 6154/5
Monday - Saturday 10.00 - 17.00 *Charge*

BRITISH LIBRARY, THE D4 26
96 Euston Rd. NW1. Not an attractive exterior but the brickwork does blend with the superb station adjacent. In the forecourt is an imposing bronze statue representing Sir Isaac Newton reducing the universe to mathematical dimensions, by Sir Eduardo Paolozzi. The library holds millions of books and manuscripts. It is a library of deposit: it receives a copy of every publication printed in Britain. Many works of art are on display throughout the library including in the entrance hall a marble statue of *Shakespeare* by Roubiliac dated 1758. There are three exhibition galleries where you will find treasures like the 7th century *Lindisfarne Gospels* (beautiful Celtic illuminated manuscripts), the *Magna Carta*, the *Gutenberg Bible* (the first printed book), and a 16th century Mercator Atlas.
Daily 9.30-18.00, Tuesday 20.00, Sats 17.00. Suns 11.00-17.00 *Free*

BENJAMIN FRANKLIN HOUSE E6 35
36 Craven St. WC2 Franklin - a scientist, an inventor, philosopher, and diplomat - was one of the most talented founders of the United States, he lived and worked here from 1757-75. The house built in 1730 in effect was the first US Embassy. *Weds-Suns 12.00-17.00 Charge*

BUCKINGHAM PALACE A3 42
The Mall, SW1. The London residence of the Queen the forecourt of which is guarded by the colourful sentries of the Guards Division, and the scene of the daily ceremony of The Changing of the Guard. *Daily May - August 11.30, weather permitting. Alternate days September - April.*
On August 7th 1993, the Queen for the first time opened the Palace State Apartments to the public. Designed by John Nash for George IV in 1826, the apartments contain beautiful brocades, furniture, clocks and paintings. The ticket office is in the Mall near the Victoria Memorial, on the Green Park side by Constitution Hill. Advance booking advisable. *Open from 7th August 9.45 - 18.30 approximately until the end of September.* *Charge*

CHESHIRE CHEESE, YE OLDE B3 36
Wine Office Court, Fleet St. EC4. An ancient hostelry, rebuilt 1667, said to have been frequented by Dr. Samuel Johnson, Goldsmith and many other literary celebrities. Sawdust, uneven floors and a mention in Dickens's *Tale of Two Cities*.

CHURCHILL WAR ROOMS D3 42
Clive Steps, King Charles St. SW1. The famous Map Room and the 21-roomed bunker and nerve centre used by Winston Churchill and his cabinet during World War Two: preserved with sound effects. *Daily April - August 9.30 - 18.00, September - March inclusive 10.00 - 18.00. Charge*

CHURCHES OF INTEREST
ALL HALLOWS BY THE TOWER B4 52
Byward Street, EC3. A church was founded here in AD 675, but the present restored building dates from the 13th and 15th centuries. The church registers record the baptism of William Penn and the marriage of John Quincy Adams, later the sixth president of the United States. There are some good brasses in this church.

BROMPTON ORATORY C5 40
Brompton Road, SW7. The London oratory of St. Philip Neri. A Roman Catholic church with a wide nave built in the Baroque style in 1884, and noted for its music and choral recitals.

ST. BARTHOLOMEW THE GREAT C2 36
West Smithfield, EC1. An interesting and historic Norman building, once an Augustinian priory, and the second oldest church in London. Unfortunately the nave was a victim of the Dissolution and today it is nowhere near its original length. At one period, the Lady Chapel was used as a print shop where Benjamin Franklin came to work. The painter Hogarth, who lived nearby, was baptised here.

ST. HELEN'S, BISHOPSGATE H3 37
Great St. Helen's., EC3. A survivor of the blitz, the Fire of London and an IRA bomb attack in 1993; this is one of the most pleasurable of the city churches. The 13th century nun's church has parallel naves, indicating that there were two churches - one was a benedictine nunnery. The church contains many monuments to city worthies, and is well known for its music.

ST. MARTIN-IN-THE-FIELDS E6 35
Trafalgar Square, WC2. Dating from 1726 this influential work by James Gibb has a temple portico and a 185 foot steeple; inside there is some very fine Italian plasterwork on the ceiling. Renowned for excellent free lunchtime concerts, winter candlelit concerts, brass rubbing and for the Café in the Crypt.

ST. PAUL'S, COVENT GARDEN E5 35
Covent Garden, WC2. Many parts of the Covent Garden area were owned by the Earl of Bedford: he commisioned Inigo Jones to build the Piazza and the church which dates from 1638, although it has been altered slightly when it was restored. Known as the 'Actors Church', there are many memorials to entertainment personalities: Charles Cochrane, Ivor Novello, Vivien Leigh, Noel Coward, Boris Karloff.

SOUTHWARK CATHEDRAL F6 37
Montague Close, SE1. A fine Gothic building that is second only to Westminster Abbey; the choir and chapel were built in 1207. Near the Shakespeare memorial is a stained-glass window depicting scenes from his plays. John Harvard, the founder of the American University, was baptised here in 1607: a chapel is dedicated to him. The new Chapter House contains a Pizza Express restaurant.

CLEOPATRA'S NEEDLE F6 35
Victoria Embankment, WC2. A pink granite obelisk 68 feet high, presented by the Egyptian viceroy in 1819, and floated here by sea in 1878. With a companion monolith in Central Park, New York, it stood at Heliopolis in 1500 BC.

DR. JOHNSON'S HOUSE — A3 36
17 Gough Square, EC4. The great man lived here from 1748 to 1759 where he wrote many of his works including his great Dictionary. *Mon - Sat 11.00 - 17.30 Charge*

ELEANOR CROSS — E6 35
Charing X Station, WC2. Many Gothic crosses were erected by Edward 1 where Queen Eleanor's coffin was set down on its route to Westminster. This Victorian replica stands east of the original location.

FLEET STREET — A4 36
EC4. Named after the old Fleet River, now a sewer running from Hampstead to Blackfriars into the Thames. It was "The Street of Ink." The newspapers have all gone now, but the street still has character.

GEORGE INN — F2 45
77 Borough High St. SE1. The surviving example of an old galleried inn well worth a visit. Famous as a coaching terminus in the 18th-19th centuries, it has a good restaurant with atmosphere.

GRAY'S INN — H1 35
Gray's Inn Rd. WC2. London has four great Inns of Court with the right to admit lawyers to practise as barristers in the English courts. They are Middle Temple, Inner Temple, Lincoln's Inn and Gray's Inn. *Monday - Friday 10.00 - 16.00. Gardens 12.00 - 14.00.*

GUILDHALL — E3 37
Gresham Street, Cheapside, EC2. For more than 800 years the centre of civic government; the first mayor was elected in 1192. Begun in about 1411, only part of the walls, the Great Hall and crypt have survived. The Great Hall with monuments of famous people is used for the election of the Lord Mayor and Sheriffs. The eastern half of the 15th century crypt is notable for its six clustered pillars of blue Purbeck marble. A new building adjoining now houses: **The Guildhall Art Gallery** which displays works from the 16c to the present day: unearthed during building are the remains of a Roman amphitheatre. *Mon - Sats 10.00 - 17.00, Suns 12.00 - 16.00 Free* The **Library** has a unique collection of prints and books on the history of the city and also contains the **Clockmakers Museum**. *Open from 9.30 - 17.00 Monday - Saturday Free*

HMS BELFAST — B5 52
Symons Wharf, Vine Lane, SE1. A famous World War Two cruiser permanently moored near Tower Bridge. Part of the Imperial War Museum the 11,500-ton cruiser played a leading role in European waters. *March - Oct. 10 - 18.00, Nov-Feb closes 16.00. Charge*

HORSE GUARDS — E1 43

Whitehall, SW1.
The Horse Guards building with its handsome clocktower was built in 1753. Here you see mounted sentries of the Household Cavalry: the Life Guards (scarlet tunics) and the Blues and Royals (blue tunics). The spectacle of the 'Changing of the Guard', takes place at 11.00 weekdays and 10.00 on Sundays. Approached through the archway is the extensive open drill ground Horse Guards Parade, which is the scene of the annual Trooping of the Colour ceremony before the Queen in early June.

HOUSES OF PARLIAMENT — E3 43
Palace of Westminster, SW1. The supreme legislature of the United Kingdom, a late-Gothic style building designed by Sir Charles Barry on the site of the former royal palace. The House of Lords, a lavishly decorated Gothic chamber, contains the throne of the Sovereign, the Woolsack, the seat of the Lord Chancellor and red leather benches for the peers. The House of Commons, rebuilt after war damage in its original style, has the Speakers chair and parallel rows of green leather benches for members. In the large Victoria Tower-336 feet to the pinnacles - are stored many Parliamentary records. A part of the old 14th century Palace of Westminster to survive is Westminster Hall, which is renowned for its hammer-beam roof - it has been the scene of great historic events and trials.

Big Ben the Clock Tower, rising to 320 feet has four dials and houses the famous fourteen-ton bell which is struck hourly. When parliament is sitting there is a light above the clock. *Book well in advance to see Prime Minister's Question Time 12.00 - 12.30 on Wednesdays. Queue for debates Mon-Thurs and some Fridays. Summer recess tours Mon-Sat 9.15-16.30 Book on ☎ 0844 847 1672*

JEWEL TOWER — E4 43
Old Palace Yard, SW1. Another survival from the old Palace of Westminster built originally to house the King's private wealth and so used until the death of Henry VIII. Now a museum showing relics of the old palace and an exhibition of Parliament's history with a video. *Daily April - October 10.00 - 17.00, November - March Sat & Sun 10.00 - 16.00 Charge*

KENSINGTON PALACE — F2 39
Kensington Palace Gdns. W8. A Jacobean building, the former residence of the Sovereign from 1689 to 1760 and later altered as the home of George 1. Many of the apartments are used for relatives of the royal family. The State Apartments include rooms by Wren and Kent, with portraits, furniture, the royal dress collection and mementoes of Queen Victoria and Queen Mary, both of whom were born in the palace. This was Princess Diana's last London residence - when they first married, Prince Charles lived here with her. *Daily Mar-Oct 10.00 - 18.00 Nov-Feb 10.00-17.00 Charge*

LAMBETH PALACE — G5 43
Lambeth Road, SE1. The official residence of the Archbishop of Canterbury for over 700 years. The famous Great Hall and other rooms contain many manuscripts and incunabula (early printed books). *Gardens are open once or twice a year Guided Tours ☎ 0844 248 5134 Charge*

LONDON BRASS RUBBING CENTRE — E6 35
St. Martins-in-the-Fields, Trafalgar Square Replicas of many fine church brasses are available for visitors to make their own brass rubbing, with instructions and the materials supplied if required. *Mon-Wed 10.00-18.00, Thurs-Sat 20.00. Sun 11.30-17.00. Charge*

LONDON EYE — G2 43
South Bank. This ferris wheel turns half-hourly. Climbing to 450 feet, the 33 capsules encompass wonderful atmospheric views over the river and London. Box Office County Hall ☎ 0871 781 3000 *Daily 10.00-20.30. May-Sept 21.30 Charge*

MADAME TUSSAUDS & STARDOME — F1 33
Marylebone Rd., NW1. Renowned waxworks exhibition with figures of the famous and infamous from the past and present. The garden party, chamber of horrors and other striking tableaux. **Stardome** the former Planetarium now explores earthly fame with a new visual experience hurtling you through space with a galaxy of stars! *Daily 9.00 - 17.30 Charge*

MANSION HOUSE — F4 37
The Lord Mayor's official residence, renowned for the magnificent Egyptian Hall used for banquets. Underneath are prison cells where Emily Pankhurst, the suffragette, was once interned.

MARBLE ARCH — E4 33
A triumphal arch at the NE corner of Hyde Park. Designed by John Nash, it was originally sited in front of Buckingham Palace, but was removed to the present position when the palace was extended. The medieval Tyburn Gallows once stood nearby.

NELSON'S COLUMN   **D6 34**
Trafalgar Square.   Monument to Lord Nelson's victory at Trafalgar in 1805. A 167 foot high fluted Corinthian column made of granite, topped by a 17 foot statue of the famous admiral. The bronze lions at the base were modelled by Sir Edwin Landseer.

OLD CURIOSITY SHOP   **G3 35**
Portsmouth Street, WC2.   In a turning off Kingsway, an antique and souvenir shop with a 16th century front, that claims to be the original *Old Curiosity Shop* made famous by Charles Dickens.

ROYAL COURTS OF JUSTICE   **H4 35**
Strand, WC2.   The Law Courts in a huge Gothic building with over 30 courts and public galleries. The Central Hall is notable for its fine rose window.

ROYAL EXCHANGE   **F4 37**
Cornhill, EC3. Sir Thomas Gresham founded the Exchange in 1566. His crest, a grasshopper, is seen as the weathervane on the 180 foot high campanile. Every three hours from 9.00 - 18.00 tunes are played on a carillon. The exchange today houses boutiques, and is a very up-market shopping centre.   *Free Monday - Friday 10.00 - 16.00, Sats 10.00 - 12.00*

ROYAL HOSPITAL, CHELSEA   **F3 49**
Royal Hospital Rd., SW3.   Founded in 1682 by Charles II for veteran and invalid soldiers. Originally designed by Wren with later building by Robert Adam and Sir John Soane. The "Chelsea Pensioners", of whom there are more than 500, wear traditional uniforms of scarlet frock coat in summer and dark blue in winter. The gardens are the scene of the annual Chelsea Flower Show. *Mon - Sat 10.00 - 12.00, and 14.00 - 16.00. Free*

ROYAL MEWS   **A4 42**
Buckingham Palace Road, SW1. Entered by an impressive Classical archway, the mews were built by John Nash, and house the Queen's unique collection of automobiles, coaches and carriages, as well as the coach horses. The main attraction is the fabulous Gold State coach which has been used for every Coronation since 1820. *Open Daily April - Oct except during state visits 10.00 - 17.00. Nov-Dec, Feb - March Mon - Sat 10.00 - 16.00*   *Charge*

SAATCHI GALLERY   **E1 49**
Duke of York's HQ, King's Road, SW3 4RY
A contemporary art collection, often controversial, located in a long elegant Georgian building in Chelsea, which was previously used as a barracks. *Daily 10.00 - 18.00*   *Free*

SEALIFE LONDON AQUARIUM   **G3 43**
County Hall, SE1. A spectacular display of aquatic life, with fishes and invertebrates from all over the world, including sharks, sea scorpions, sting rays and deadly piranhas.   *Charge Mon-Thurs 10.00 - 18.00,   Fri-Sun 10.00 - 19.00*

SHAKESPEARE'S GLOBE   **D6 36**
New Globe Walk, Bankside, SE1. We have to thank American actor, Sam Wanamaker, for the persistence of his vision to rebuild the Globe near to the original site of the theatre where Shakespeare produced his plays. There is an exhibition, and during the summer the open-air theatre will demonstrate theatre as it was in Shakespeare's time. The restaurants have good river views and occasional music. *Daily 9.00 -17.00.*

Tours of the theatre are also available.   *Charge*

SHERLOCK HOLMES MUSEUM   **E6 25**
221b Baker Street, NW1. A small popular museum that makes the most out of Sir Arthur Conan Doyle's fictional character. On the ground floor is Hudson's Restaurant for tea!   *Daily 9.30 - 18.00 Charge*

SPEAKERS CORNER   **E5 33**
On the NE of Hyde Park near Marble Arch. Anyone can indulge in free speech without hindrance - other than hecklers - before a usually amused audience.

TEMPLE, THE   **A4 36**
Fleet Street, EC4. Of the four Inns of Court of the legal profession in London, two are here, Middle Temple and Inner Temple, in a quiet traffic-free oasis of lovely gardens and Georgian buildings. Here too is the Round Church, built by the Knight Templars in the 12th century on the model of the church of the Holy Sepulchre in Jerusalem, with a rectangular Early English chancel added a century later. Above the east gate is Prince Henry's Room built in 1610.

TOWER BRIDGE   **C6 52**
A unique drawbridge across the Thames - a symbol of London. The bridge's twin bascules, each weighing about 1000 tons, are between two huge Gothic towers, connected near the top by a fixed glazed walkway with panoramic views, and standing 140 feet above high water level. The central span measures 200 feet and the suspension chains on either side 270 feet. The bascules carrying the roadway are raised hydraulically to permit the passage of large vessels. *Museum Daily April - September   10.00 - 18.00. October - March 9.30 - 17.30*   *Charge*

WELLINGTON ARCH / Quadriga Gallery G2 41
Hyde Park Corner, W1. Triumphal arch built in 1828 by Decimus Burton topped by Adrian Jones's striking bronze *Peace* quadriga, or four-horse chariot. The Gallery is on the upper floors. Good views from top. *May - March, Weds - Suns 10.00-17.00 Charge*

WESLEY'S HOUSE & CHAPEL   **F6 29**
49 City Rd. EC1.   This is an 18th century chapel and Georgian town house where the founder of Methodism lived. Mrs Thatcher got married here! *Mons - Sats 10.00 - 16.00, Suns 12.30-13.45.   Free*

WESTMINSTER ABBEY   **E4 43**
Parliament Square, SW1.
Subject to the Sovereign, not the church through a dean and chapter, the Abbey has been the crowning place of all[*] of the English monarchs since William the Conqueror: here too most of them since Henry III are buried. There are tombs and monuments to statesmen, warriors, poets and men of letters. Of interest is the Coronation Chair, made for Edward I, and the Stone of Scone beneath, and upon which the Kings of Scotland and every[*] English monarch since Edward I have been crowned. Poets' Corner is in the South Transept. The *Grave of the Unknown Warrior* is just inside the West Door. Once meeting place of the House of Commons, the Chapter House dates from 1250. The architect of the west towers was Nicholas Hawksmoor, a pupil of Wren. They date from 1745. *Mon, Tues, Thurs, Fris 9.30-16.30, Weds 19.00, Sats 9.30-14.30*   *Charge*

WESTMINSTER CATHEDRAL   **B5 42**
Ashley Place, SW1. The central Roman Catholic church in England. Seat of the Cardinal Archbishop of Westminster. A very large church constructed in 1903 in the Early Byzantine and the Romanesque styles with a pleasant piazza frontage. Built in alternate layers of red brick and portland stone it has a pleasing and unusual effect. The campanile, or tower is 273 feet high. *Daily 7.00-20.00. Charge to ascend the tower.*

[*]All but two - the boy king Edward V murdered in the Tower and Edward VIII later the Duke of Windsor.[*]

CHRISTOPHER WREN'S LONDON

Christopher Wren was born in East Knoyle, Wiltshire in 1632. He went to Westminster School and then Oxford at the age of fourteen, where he studied mathematics and where later, at the age of 28, he became the Professor of Astronomy. In 1665, he spent six months in Paris studying architecture, the following year his opportunity came after the Fire of London had destroyed the city. He was asked to be the Surveyor-General and to prepare a master plan for the reconstruction of London. Unfortunately people began building very quickly and his plan for the whole city was not used: even today, the city is a haphazard muddle of buildings and alleys. We can only guess at the elegance and space his plan would have brought by marvelling at his great achievements: St Paul's and Greenwich Hospital in London, and the Sheldonian theatre in Oxford. These reach heights of dignity and classicism which have set the standards in English Architecture. Wren lived until 1723; he was 91 when he died, proof that work kills nobody.

MONUMENT, THE   A4 52
Fish Street Hill, EC3.   Wren built this 62 metre (202 feet) high fluted Doric column in portland stone between 1671-7, to commemorate the Great Fire of 1666, which broke out in Pudding Lane nearby. Some 311 steps lead up to a caged balcony - underneath a spiky ball - from which there are some great views of the city. *Charge Daily 9.30 - 17.30 Last admission 17.00*

ST PAUL'S CATHEDRAL   D4 36

St Paul's Churchyard, EC4. Wren's majestic masterpiece, the largest and most famous church in London. The beautiful dome reaches to a height of 110 metres (365ft), and within the dome is the whispering gallery which has some quite amazing acoustic properties - try it out! Wren was 43 when the foundation stone was laid, and 79 when it was finished. The money to build the cathedral was raised by an importation tax on coal and wine coming in through London's docks. Wren's sojourn in Paris quite clearly helped him to formulate his inspiration and enthusiasm for classical and renaissance architecture. His first model of the cathedral - which when rejected they say brought him to tears - can be viewed in the Trophy Room in the Triforium. The dome ceiling was painted by James Thornhill who was nearly killed executing his work, which depicts the life of St Paul. In the Crypt there are numerous tombs of famous men including Wren, Nelson, and Wellington, and also a memorial to Lawrence of Arabia.
Many people will want to see *The Light of the World* by Holman Hunt, the Pre-Raphaelite painter; this is in the nave. In the south choir aisle is the only monument from medieval St Paul's that survived the fire, the tomb of the Poet-Dean John Donne, 'No man is an Island...' his love poems live on to this day. Only the young in heart and body should attempt the experience of climbing to the top; you can go just underneath the ball and cross, there are 628 steps for you to mount - count them!
Monday - Saturday 8.30 - 16.00.   *Charge*

There is no doubt at all that Christopher Wren was a great architect. However much doubt has been cast by hand-writing experts over the past few years as to whether he was responsible for so many of London's city churches. The fact that a Wren church equals a tourist attraction is probably responsible for the myths. As the surveyor-general, he must have been the overall supervisor, but as for the nitty-gritties, he would surely have delegated to those working in his office to get so much work done in such a short time. Here is a list of churches in chronological order:
ST MICHAEL, Cornhill. 1670-2.   **G4 37**
The nave is attributed to Wren.
ST VEDAST, Foster Lane. 1670-3.   **D3 36**
ST MARY AT HILL, St.Mary at Hill. 1670-6 **G5 37**
ST MARY-LE-BOW, Cheapside.1670-83   **E4 37**
Damaged by the luftwaffe, Bow Church - the original cockney church - was restored after the war; the original *Bow Bells* as the story goes, recalled Dick Whittington as Lord Mayor.
ST LAWRENCE, Gresham St. 1671-7   **E3 37**
ST BRIDE'S, Fleet Street. 1671-1703.   **B4 36**
When it was blitzed in 1941, Roman and Saxon remains were discovered; these can be viewed in the crypt. The telescopic steeple (68 metres or 226 feet) is Wren's tallest parish church steeple.It is said that it has been the blueprint for many wedding cakes!
ST MAGNUS, Lower Thames St.,1671-1705. **G5 37**
ST STEPHEN WALBROOK, 1672-1717.   **F4 37**
Many people regard this church as his finest - a mini St. Paul's. The Samaritans - who help people through their problems by listening - were founded here in 1953 by the rector Chad Varah; the poignant memorial to him is a telephone in a glass box. Another recent addition is the central white stone altar by Henry Moore.
ST JAMES, Garlick Hill. 1674-87.   **E5 37**
ST ANNE & ST AGNES,   **D3 36**
Gresham St.1677-80.
ST BENET, Upper Thames St. 1677-83.   **D5 36**
Said to be the work of Robert Hooke, a junior who worked in Wren's office, it somewhat resembles a Dutch church.
CHRIST CHURCH, Newgate St. 1677-87.   **C3 36**
The stylish tower is all that remains.
ST MARTIN, Ludgate Hill.1677-87.   **C4 36**
ST PETER, Cornhill. 1677-87   **G4 37**
ST CLEMENT DANES, Strand. 1680-2   **H4 35**
The Airforce church with a statue of the controversial Bomber Harris standing outside. James Gibbs, the architect of St.Martin-in-the-Fields and a great follower of Wren, finished the spire. He was also responsible for St.Mary-le-Strand (G4 35) which is now located on a traffic island.
ST MARY, Abchurch Lane.1681-6.   **F4 37**
A ceiling painted by James Thornhill.
ST MARY, Aldermary, Queen Victoria St. **E4 37**
1681-1704. Re-interpreted Gothic-style church.
ST JAMES, Piccadilly. (1682-84)   **B6 34**
A small parish church for Wren, not the site of a building damaged in the Great Fire. Bombed in WW2: now beautifully restored. Famous today for free lunchtime concerts and the daily craft market.
ST CLEMENT, Clements Lane. 1683-87   **F5 37**
ST MARGARET, Eastcheap 1684-89   **G5 37**
ST ANDREW, Queen Victoria St. 1685-95 **C4 36**
ST MARGARET, Lothbury. 1686-90   **F3 37**
ST MICHAEL, College Hill, 1686-94   **E5 37**
There were many other fine churches built by Wren that have now disappeared due to bombing in the Second World War. On the south side of the Thames in Bankside (D6 36) opposite St.Paul's is a house that some say he lived in - see the plaque!

GREENWICH

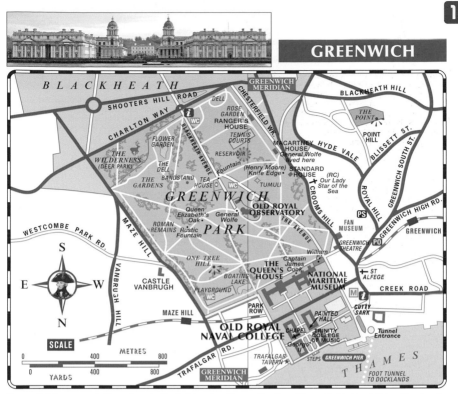

Greenwich is a marvel. It so close to Central London (four miles from Tower Bridge), yet it has the air of a picturesque fishing village. Contrary, it also has probably the finest Classical - Baroque display of architecture in the country, by some of England's greatest architects: Inigo Jones, Christopher Wren, John Webb and Nicholas Hawksmoor. The best way to reach Greenwich is by river boat: there are cruises from Westminster, Charing Cross and Tower Piers. Alternatively, the Docklands Light Railway will take you to Island Gardens where you can walk across under the Thames (lifts take you down to the tunnel). The atmospheric view of the Naval College from Island Gardens is incomparable, particularly on a nice evening. On Saturdays and Sundays there is a very good Arts and Crafts market (see map) in the historic covered market.

OLD ROYAL NAVAL COLLEGE Originally built as a Hospital for sailors between 1664-1702. The West river fronting building was by John Webb, and then Wren produced the plan we now see, incorporating the original building into the grand plan. **The Painted Hall** Arguably England's finest secular interior, designed by Nicholas Hawksmoor in the Baroque style, with marvellous paintings by James Thornhill, who painted the ceiling of St.Paul's. You can wheel a mirror trolley around to save craning your neck to view the painting - well worth seeing and it is free. It was after Trafalgar that Nelson's body was brought to lie in state. **The Chapel** was designed by Wren and Ripley and completed after Wren died. It is interesting to note that the two busts on each side of the door are of 'Kiss me' Hardy, a friend of Nelson and the poet Keats. Hardy was also a 'Shipmate' of the Sailor King, William IV! *Daily 10.00 - 17.00.* *Free*

CUTTY SARK Now a museum the famous tea clipper was launched in 1869 - the same year that the Suez Canal opened. The ship broke records ploughing her way to and from China bringing back cargoes of tea; in later years she carried wool from Newcastle in Australia. After a devastating fire in 2007 the ship has been lovingly restored. *Open Daily 10.00-17.00 Charge*

THE NATIONAL MARITIME MUSEUM Very much devoted to Nelson and his historic achievements, there is a huge painting by Turner of the battle of Trafalgar. Of course that is not all: there are sections for Francis Drake, the practical Captain Cook and for John Franklin, whose name is recorded on maps of North America for posterity, reminding us of his relentless voyages to find the Northwest Passage.

The Queen's House A 17th century Palladian style villa by Inigo Jones that preceded everything else on the site. The wings were added after Trafalgar. The 'Tulip Staircase' is the star feature of the house. *Daily 10.00 - 17.00.* *Free*

ST. ALFEGE This is a church by Hawksmoor. Like a temple in concept. General Wolfe was buried here.

OLD ROYAL OBSERVATORY Built by Christopher Wren, it now houses the Museum of Astronomy. To the left of the gates is the Meridian Building, which since 1884 has been the starting point of global measurement for time and space - the 'Prime Meridian'.The red *time-ball* rises every day at 13.00. *Daily 10.00-17.00. Free*

GREENWICH PARK Open from dawn until dusk, and originally laid out by Le Nôtre, of Versailles fame. The park is full of interest: a magnificent statue of General Wolfe at the top of the hill (a great place to take photos), Henry Moore sculpture, the remains of a Roman Temple, and a Deer Park are just a few of the features to look out for.

ENTERTAINMENTS

London is world renowned for excellent and varied entertainments, especially music and theatre. For details the Saturday *Guardian* newspaper has a free supplement.There are also many free listing papers that you might find in your hotel lobby. *Time Out* publish a listing magazine, and there is always the *Big Issue* which helps the homeless.

Concert Halls

BARBICAN HALL E1 37
Silk Street, EC2. ☎ 7638 8891
This is the spiritual home of the London Symphony Orchestra. The hall also plays host to some of the leading orchestras in the world. Seating over 2000, with good sight lines and acoustics that have been improved over the years.

ROYAL ALBERT HALL A3 40
Kensington Gore, SW7. ☎ 7589 8212
Built in 1871 as a memorial to the Prince Consort,

this huge, beautiful amphitheatre with a dome of iron and glass can hold over 8000 within its circumference. The hall is not only used for classical music; there are all kinds of entertainment and sports held here. But it is the summertime Promenade Concerts which endears it to Londoners. The programmes of the *Proms* are always diverse and interesting (compared with the average concert). The last night is a memorable festive occasion. The organ is tremendous - I once remember nearly falling off my seat when the organ entered at the start of the Poulenc organ concerto!

CADOGAN HALL F6 41
5 Sloane Terrace, SW1 ☎ 7730 4500
The building with a Byzantine style tower was formerly a church; now a concert venue, and the home of the Royal Philharmonic orchestra. Eclectic programming, good acoustics and a very intimate atmosphere are a feature.

ROYAL FESTIVAL HALL G1 43
South Bank, SE1. ☎ 7960 4242
Described by Aram Khachaturian as a large wheat granary when it was built for the Festival of Britain way back in 1951, this 2600 seat hall with its elm panels and excellent acoustics is still going strong after a major refurbishment. During intervals you can walk around the terrace and view the river.
Queen Elizabeth Hall Situated close by, with less than half the capacity of the Festival Hall, this is a more intimate venue suited for small orchestras or jazz orientated music.
Purcell Room Even smaller still; this is an ideal place to hear a piano recital or small jazz combo. The Queen Elizabeth and the Purcell Room are both comfortable venues, but the exteriors are very stark indeed which is unfortunate.

WIGMORE HALL H3 33
Wigmore Street, W1. ☎ 7935 2141
An elegant hall with plenty of marble and alabaster, forever linked with the piano manufacturer Bechstein who had the hall built to showcase his pianos (his shop was next door). It is a comfortable place for classical and jazz music, with very good acoustics.

ST.JOHN'S, SMITH SQUARE E5 43
Smith Square, SW1. ☎ 7222 1061
Used by the BBC for its lunchtime chamber concerts, this Baroque building is a popular venue for the office workers in the Westminster area.

Opera and Ballet

As a small boy my mother deposited me outside Sadlers Wells into the care of a school teacher friend for my initiation into Opera. I did not want to go and never said I enjoyed the experience. I did though, and I have loved Opera ever since. Opera today is very expensive and unfortunately a good seat for Covent Garden makes it a very special occasion. The English National Opera and Sadlers Wells are less expensive and they do have some very adventurous productions in very good theatres.

LONDON COLISEUM E5 35
St.Martin's Lane, WC2. ☎ 7632 8300
The flashing globe makes this 1904 Romansque style theatre instantly recognisable. Built by Oswald Stoll, it is very large (2350 seats) and is the home of the English National Opera. Opulent and inviting, this theatre is the place to see not only ENO but visiting opera and ballet companies. Lily Langtry and the famous Ballet Russe performed on this stage.

OPERA HOLLAND PARK C3 38
Holland Park, W8. ☎ 7602 7856
During the summer months you can see Opera and Ballet with a good standard of production performed under a large canopy in Holland Park. Previous productions include *Tosca* and *Eugene Onegin*.

ROYAL OPERA HOUSE F4 35
Covent Garden, WC2. ☎ 7304 4000
Preceeded by two other theatres, both destroyed by fire, this one dates from 1858 and is not only the home of the Royal Opera, but also the Royal Ballet. Situated in an attractive location it is now adjoined at the side to the small Linbury Studio Theatre and is much more accessible than it used to be. If you anticipate seeing a production I recommend the ballet, it is usually cheaper and the theatre is a lovely experience.

SADLER'S WELLS B4 28
Rosebery Avenue, EC1 ☎ 7863 8000

Eclectic in its dance, opera and lyric programming, Sadler's Wells was never only accessible to the elite; the drawbacks were a small, sloping stage and a vestibule that was almost on the pavement. Now we have London's first new theatre of the 21st century; a great improvement, and a place to see the very best in international arts. Even the walls and ceiling surfaces can become an extension of the scenery and imagery on the stage.

Ticket Agencies

TKTS Booth D5 34
Half Price Tickets with a small service charge are available for same day London West End productions from the booth situated on the south side of Leicester Square by the gardens. Open Monday to Saturday. *Matinees 12.00 - 14.00, Evening 14.00 - 18.30.*

KEITH PROWSE tickets ☎ 0870 840 1111
24 Hour Credit Card Booking for London theatres, some cinemas, and South Bank Concerts etc. They also provide tickets for events throughout the world.

BRITAIN & LONDON VISITOR CENTRE C6 34
Situated in Lower Regent's Street, tickets can be booked for West End shows.

TICKETMASTER ☎ 0870 154 4040
Credit Card Booking for London shows, sports events, concerts etc. 24 Hour Booking.

Theatres

West End theatre is Shaftesbury Avenue; this is Theatreland. However, it spreads much wider now with the Barbican Centre and the South Bank contributing to the scene. London has only one rival in the world - Broadway. Here are a few theatres that I like and which might be of interest to you for their productions, architecture or decor.

ALMEIDA   **B1 28**
Almeida Street, N1.   ☎ 7359 4404
Situated in Islington, stars come here to act in its productions. Completely refurbished in 2003. Pinter plays have been premiered here.

AMBASSADORS   **D4 34**
West Street, WC2.   ☎ 7836 1171
Agatha Christie's The Mousetrap has played here since 1952 - what more can you say!

APOLLO VICTORIA   **A5 42**
Wilton Road, SW1.   ☎ 7630 6262
A large theatre and foyer built as a cinema in the 1930's. The theatre still retains its original almost subterranean decor, although the colouring which was blue and green has been altered.

BARBICAN   **E1 37**
Barbican Centre, EC2.   ☎ 7638 8891
An eclectic mix of productions from Shakespeare to musicals like 'South Pacific'. Although it has a large capacity all the seats are close to the stage. The Barbican Centre is also worth exploring.

HAYMARKET   **D6 34**
Haymarket,SW1.   ☎ 7930 8800
An 1831 theatre designed by John Nash. An ornate auditorium that saw the premieres of a number of Oscar Wilde plays.

HER MAJESTY'S   **D6 34**
Haymarket, SW1.   ☎ 7494 5400
Opened in 1897, the theatre had great success when it introduced Bernard Shaw's Pygmalion. In more recent times it staged the National's Amadeus and Andrew Lloyd Webber's Phantom of the Opera.

ROYAL NATIONAL THEATRE   **H6 35**
South Bank, SE1. ☎ 7928 2252
Comprising of three theatres, the Olivier, Lyttelton and Cottesloe (in order of size). The buildings here with the Hayward Gallery always give me the feeling that Stalin will appear on the balcony. However the productions are excellent, and inside the buildings are spacious and comfortable.

OPEN AIR THEATRE   **F4 25**
Regent's Park, Inner Circle, NW1.   ☎ 7486 2431
One of the joys of summer are my annual visits to this theatre. Alfresco it is, so take an umbrella and something for a chilly evening. If you have never seen A Midsummer Nights Dream this is the perfect place - it is magical. Good buffet food underneath the amphitheatre and you can bring your own wine.

LONDON PALLADIUM   **B4 34**
Argyll Street W1.   ☎ 7494 5020
Designed as a music hall in 1910. The top names have all played here: Judy Garland, Danny Kaye, Frank Sinatra and Irving Berlin with his This Is The Army show. The ticket office wall is lined with posters demonstrating the fact that this was, and is, the mecca of light entertainment.

THEATRE ROYAL DRURY LANE   **F4 35**
Catherine Street, SW1.   ☎ 7494 5000
Two other theatres have stood on this site since the time of Charles II. This one dates from 1812 and is the largest theatre in London. Over the years many musical productions - Oklahoma, Carousel, My Fair Lady, and Miss Saigon - have been staged here.

Cinemas

Most of London's cinemas have lost their glamour. The demand for choice has divided up the buildings so unless they were purpose built, the great decors appear to have gone. Here are some where you might care to see a good film.

BFI SOUTHBANK   **H1 43**
South Bank, SE1.   ☎ 7928 3232
Underneath Waterloo bridge, this is a repertory cinema, changing daily and showing great films and classics - Eisenstein through to Tarentino.

CURZON MAYFAIR   **G1 41**
Curzon Street, W1.   ☎ 7369 1720
Real armchair comfort in the heart of Mayfair with programs featuring foreign and art films.

EMPIRE   **D5 34**
Leicester Square, WC2.   ☎ 0870 010 2030
Empire One is a good place to see a wide screen epic. My parents first date was in this cinema; if I tell you that the star was Lew Ayres, guess the film.

ODEON   **D5 34**
Leicester Square WC2.   ☎ 0870 505 0007
The largest ordinary screen and cinema in the metropolis. It is used for premieres, when celebrities bring panache to the occasions.

BFI LONDON IMAX   **H1 43**
Waterloo Rd. SE1.   ☎ 7902 1234
The largest screen in Great Britain, the place for a cinematic experience, rather than the latest film.

Jazz in London

Jazz in London is thriving. Some older clubs are still around, and thanks to the Pizza Express chain policy of providing jazz in their restaurants, venues have increased. Ronnie Scott's (D4 34) does not need an introduction: the perfect club, if only the clientele were real jazz fans. My memories apart from the late Ronnie Scott's jokes include standing next to Jane Russell in the vestibule: she had come to hear her friend, Anita O'Day (the lady with the hat in the film, Jazz on a Summers Day). Another extremely poignant memory was seeing Bill Evans two weeks before he died. From 12.00-16.00 on Sundays there is a Lunch Show.
The Pizza Express in Dean Street (C3 34) and in King's Road Chelsea at the Pheasantry (D2 48) both offer a menu of mainstream jazz and are highly recommended. The 100 Club (C3 34) in Oxford Street has been going so long it is amazing. The traditional, blues, soul and dixieland music are accompanied here by a menu of simple food. Reasonable admission charges.
I like the 606 Club (H6 47) in Chelsea; gourmet food, good modern jazz and it opens for seven days a week. The Jazz Cafe (D6 23) in a former bank building in Camden Town, offers the best in modern music and jazz and attracts some great musicians like Bobby Watson, José Feliciano. Often over the Christmas period, the place gently rocks to the music of the London Community Gospel Choir.

> **THE BULL'S HEAD** On the southside of the river Thames near Barnes Bridge in Lonsdale Road, this pub has served jazz with excellent beer every day for many years. All the best musicians love the place; the audience is usually appreciative, and the music eclectic. Get a train from Waterloo to Barnes Bridge Station and walk about 30 yards, or go by the tube to Hammersmith and catch a 209 bus in the terminal to Barnes Bridge.

SERVICES AND USEFUL INFORMATION

Information Centres

☎ Prefix numbers with **020** when dialling from outside CENTRAL LONDON

City of London Information Centre *i*
St.Paul's Churchyard, EC4
www.visitthecity.co.uk ☎ *020 7332 1456*
VISIT LONDON
Telephone Information Service ☎ *08701 566 366*
www.visitlondon.com
Travel Information Centres *i*
Euston Station, 8.15 - 19.15, Sun 20.15
King's Cross St. Pancras
7.15-21.15, Sun 8.15-20.15
Liverpool St. 8.15-19.15, Sun 20.15
Victoria Station, 7.15-21.15, *Sun 8.15 - 19.15*.
Piccadilly Circus, located in the underground
station 9.15-19.00

AIR TRAVEL
GATWICK *(flight enquiries)* ☎ *0870 000 2468*
HEATHROW ☎ *0870 000 0123*
LUTON ☎ *01582 405 100*
STANSTED ☎ *0870 0000 303*
LONDON CITY ☎ *020 7646 0000*
BRITISH AIRWAYS
Customer Service ☎ 0844 *493 0787*
HEATHROW EXPRESS at
Paddington Station, W2 ☎ *0845 600 1515*

WEATHER FORECAST ☎ *0906 850 0401*
DOCKLANDS LIGHT RAILWAY
Docklands Travel Hotline ☎ *020 7918 4000*
Travel Check ☎ *020 7222 1200*

Emergency Services

AMBULANCE, FIRE, POLICE ☎ *Dial 999*
MEDICAL SERVICE
University College Hospital
Gower Street, W1 [A&E]
St Thomas' Hospital
Westminster Bridge Road SE1
DENTAL SERVICE
Eastman Dental Hospital
256 Gray's Inn Road, WC1X
Mondays to Fridays 09.00 - 16.00
Outside these hours go to a General Hospital.
EYE TREATMENT
Moorfields Eye Hospital
City Road, EC1
TRAFALGAR SQUARE POST OFFICE
William V Street, Trafalgar Square, WC2. [PO]
Mondays to Saturdays 08.00 - 20.00
LOST PROPERTY
For property lost in taxis or on the street apply to
any Police Station.
In Underground trains, buses and taxis apply
TfL Lost Property Office: 200 Baker Street, NW1.
Mon-Fri 8.30-16.00, except Bank Holidays
In Main Line Trains, contact the station master at
departure or destination stations.
In Department Stores, Hotels, Airports contact the
premises in question.
LATE OPENING CHEMISTS
Chemists in London districts work on a rotating
system for late opening. The lists are always
posted on the door or window. Otherwise the
local Police Station will have the information.

⚡ **ELECTRICITY** ⚡ 220/240 Volts with 3 pin plugs.
Shavers sockets have 2 thick round pins - do not use
any other appliance in these sockets!

AIRPORT TRANSFER
Heathrow The Piccadilly Underground Station
at Heathrow takes you into the centre of London.
The Heathrow Express runs every 15 minutes
from Paddington Station (full check-in facility for
20 airlines) taking 20 minutes. ☎ *0845 600 1515*
Gatwick The Gatwick Express runs to and from
Victoria Station 04.30-06.00 and 20.00-00.30
every 30 minutes, from 06.00-20.00 it runs every
15 minutes. Allow approximately 35 minutes for
the journey ☎ *0845 850 1530*
Stansted The Easybus operates to and from
Baker Street, the journey time is approx. one hour
15 minutes.
nationalexpress operates to and from the airport
to Victoria Coach Station, the journey takes approx.
90 minutes, they also go to and from Liverpool
Street Station. ☎ *0870 580 8080*

BANKING HOURS
Banking hours are from 09.30-15.30 (although
many now stay open until 17.00) Mondays to
Fridays. However some of the larger department
stores have banks and these remain open during
trading hours. Most banks have cash machines
outside available at all hours.

CREDIT CARDS
Most large shops, department stores, hotels and
restaurants will accept international credit cards
such as American Express, Diners' Club, Eurocard,
Mastercard and Visa etc.

PUBLIC HOLIDAYS
New Years Day January 1st
Good Friday (late March early April)
May Day (the first Monday)
Spring Bank Holiday last Monday in May
Summer Bank Holiday last Monday in August
Christmas Day December 25th
Boxing Day December 26th

INTERNATIONAL TELEPHONE CALLS
To make an international call dial 00 then dial the
Country Code followed by the individual number.
To make a call to London from outside the United
Kingdom dial the international code then 44.

TELEPHONE DIRECTORY ENQUIRIES
118 500 for numbers in the United Kingdom.
118 505 for International Numbers.
From a Public Call Box this service is free

CLOTHING and SHOE SIZES approximate

SHIRTS							
Europe	36	37	38	39	40	41	42
UK and USA	14	14.5	15	15.5	16	16.5	17

DRESSES							
Europe	36	38	40	42	44	46	48
UK	8	10	12	14	16	18	20
USA	6	8	10	12	14	16	18

MEN'S SHOES							
Europe	39	40	41	42	43	44	45
UK and USA	6	7	7.5	8.5	9	10	11

WOMEN'S SHOES							
Europe	35.5	36	36.5	37	37.5	38	39
UK	3	3.5	4	4.5	5	5.5	6
USA	4.5	5	5.5	6	6.5	7	7.5

SHOPPING

People come from all over the world to shop in London and justifiably so, with two of the world's most celebrated department stores - Harrod's and Selfridges - and all kinds of shops and markets for any size of pocket. Off the map (Page 38 A2-3) is London's newest & largest shopping mall - Westfield.

Shopping Areas

BOND STREET A5 34
Divided in two sections - Old Bond Street and New Bond street. A street of fashionable shops and fine art dealers, with many respected names in fashion. Fenwick's department store, and home to Sotheby's the auctioneers.

BURLINGTON ARCADE B6 34
Running into Piccadilly and patrolled by uniformed beadles, it is very expensive but exquisite! Elegant specialist shops sell, silver, jewellery and knitwear.

CARNABY STREET B4 34
Associated with the Pop Culture and fashion of the 60s this colourful street became a legend. Today it still retains a unique atmosphere.

CHARING CROSS ROAD D3 34
A road that once never ceased to attract scholars and musicians. Although many antiquarian bookshops have gone, the unique Foyles in two buildings has survived. Music shops are on this street and in side turnings like Denmark Street.

JERMYN STREET B6 34
If you need shirts here is the place to have them made to measure. Expensive jewellery shops are here too with a perfumiers and a specialist cheesemonger.

KENSINGTON HIGH STREET D4 38
A popular shopping street for young fashions, boutiques and high-class couture, landmarked by the 1938 modernity of Barkers department store - now home to the Whole Foods Market.

KINGS ROAD, CHELSEA B3 48
Boutiques, pubs, bistros, antique dealers, and one department store on Sloane Square called Peter Jones (a John Lewis store): the other side of the road is a new shopping plaza near the Saatchi Gallery

KNIGHTSBRIDGE D3 40
Unequalled for its fashion, food and art shops. This is where to find Harrods and what was Princess Diana's favourite store, Harvey Nichols.

NEAL STREET E4 35
A relatively new thriving shopping area for young people close to Covent Garden piazza.

OXFORD STREET F4 33
London's most famous shopping street with large department stores including Selfridges, Marks & Spencer, D. H.Evans and Debenhams etc. HMV has one shop for CDs and records. Just off the street near Selfridges is St Christopher's Place (G3 33) - a pleasant eating area.

REGENT STREET B4 34
This gently curving street of noble architecture is where to find the immutable yet changing department store Liberty's and the largest toy shop in Europe, Hamley's. Disney and Warner Brothers have also congregated alongside.

TOTTENHAM COURT ROAD C1 34
Apart from the great furnishing shop Heal's, this is the home of bargain HiFi; TV; Radio; Computers and almost anything electronic. Check around before you buy and you should get a good bargain!

> **TRADING TIMES*** *Shops usually open at 9.00 and close at 18.00 Monday to Saturday, closing at 20.00 on Thursdays in the West End, Wednesdays in Knightsbridge, Sloane Square and Kings Road.*

Department Stores

FORTNUM & MASON B6 34
Respected for its provisions department, tea, coffee, jams and aristocratic sales persona etc.

HARRODS D4 40
Above all else, do not miss the Edwardian food hall; it is out of this world, undeniably one of the world's greatest stores. See the fountain memorial to Princess Diana and Dodi Fayed on the lower ground floor.

HARVEY NICHOLS E3 41
Situated in Knightsbridge, stylish and well known for vogueish fashion with a very good food hall on the top floor.

JOHN LEWIS H3 33
The Oxford Street branch is the flagship of this standardised chain. Good quality products but not as interesting as some of the other stores here.

LIBERTY B4 34
Famous for its amazing 1924 Tudor-style building and its classic fabrics. Children will enjoy the clock outside - St.George chases the dragon every 15 mins.

SELFRIDGES F4 33
Spacious and renowned for its sales, the interior has recently been renovated. Above the main entrance is a superb Art-deco clock. Almost everything you need can be bought here. Delicious tea in the restaurants when you want to rest your feet.

Markets

BERWICK STREET C4 34
Soho's busy friendly fruit & vegetable market Monday to Saturday from 5.00 am.

BRICK LANE D1 52
London's curry centre, and heart of the leather industry, odds and ends etc. Sunday mornings.

BRIXTON Off the map area in an arcade and streets near the station. Worth a visit for the exotic sunny caribbean atmosphere - absolutely marvellous, for fish. Monday to Saturday. Underground Brixton.

CAMDEN PASSAGE B2 28
Small Islington outdoor antique market,Weds & Sats.

CAMDEN MARKETS C5 23
A daily indoor market, arts, crafts, clothes etc. The outdoor market is a tourist attraction and is open from Thursday to Sunday.

CHURCH STREET B1 32
General market, good for antiques. Mons-Sats.

COVENT GARDEN F5 35
A covered market with buskers outside in the piazza to entertain you. Monday, antiques, and Tuesday to Sunday arts and crafts 9.00 - 16.00.

LEADENHALL A3 52
Classic indoor market, incorporates the famous Lamb Tavern. Meat, poultry, fish, plants. Mons - Fris.

LEATHER LANE A1 36
Lunchtime market Monday to Friday.

NEW CALEDONIAN H4 45
Quality antiques, go early. Friday 6.00 - 13.00.

PETTICOAT LANE B1 52
Famous and large street market. Sundays am.

PORTOBELLO ROAD B3 30
Boutiques, antiques, almost anything. Mons - Sats.

OLD SPITALFIELDS C1 52
Antiques and crafts weekdays 9.00 - 17.00, Fridays and Sundays organic covered market.

**Sundays many shops in Central London open from approximately 12.00 to 18.00 especially in Oxford Street.*

LEGEND - ENGLISH - FRANÇAIS - DEUTSCH - NEDERLANDS - ITALIANO - ESPAÑOL

HOSPITALS
Hôpitaux
Krankenhäus
Ziekenhuisen
Ospedali
Hospitales

St.Mary's Hospital

TOURIST INFORMATION
Informations Touristiques
Touristenauskünfte
Toeristen Informatie
Informazione Turistiche
Información Turística

POLICE STATION
Gendarmerie
Polizeiwache
Politie
Polizia
Comisaría

PS

FOOTPATH
Sentier
Fusspfad
Voetpad
Sentiero
Senda

POST OFFICE
Bureau de Poste
Postamt
Postkantoor
Ufficio Postale
Correos

PO

PUBLIC PARK
Jardin Public
Öffentliche Parkanlage
Publiek Park
Giardino Pubblico
Parque Publico

PHARMACY
Pharmacie
Apotheke
Apotheek
Farmacia
Farmácia

CEMETERY
Cimetière
Friedhof
Begraafplaats
Cimiteri
Cementerio

HOTEL
Hôtel
Hotel
Hotel
Albergo
Hotel

DORCHESTER

RAILWAY STATION
Gares
Bahnhof
Station
Stazione
Estación

(EASTERN REGION)
LIVERPOOL STREET

CHURCHES
Églises
Kirchen
Kerken
Chiese di
Iglesias

St. Helen's †

OUTDOOR STATUES and SCULPTURES
Statues et Sculptures dehors
Im Freien stehende Standbilder und Skulpturen
Standbeelden en Beeldhouwkunst buiten
Statue e Sculture all'aperto
Estatuas y Escultura al aire libre

Edith Cavell

SYNAGOGUE
Synagogue
Synagoge
Synagogen
Sinagoga
Sinagoga

✡

THEATRES and CONCERT HALLS
Théâtres et Salles de Concerts
Theater und Konzertsäle
Theaters en Concertzalen
Teatri e Sale dei Concerti
Teatros y Salas de Concertos

COLISEUM ■

JAZZ CLUB
Jazz Club
Jazz Club
Jazz Club
Jazz Club
Jazz Club

RONNIE SCOTT'S ★

CINEMA
Cinéma
Kino
Bioscoop
Cinema
Cine

EMPIRE ■

DISCO or DANCE HALL
Disco ou Salle de Danse
Disko oder Tanzsaal
Disco of Dans Zaal
Disco o Sala di Danza
Disco o Salón de Baile

The Forum ★

RESTAURANT OR CAFE
Restaurant ou Café
Restaurant oder Cafe
Restaurant of Café
Ristorante o Cafe
Restorant o Cafe

Le Tour de la Pont ●

BUS ROUTE TERMINUS
Terminus d'Autobus
Endstation, Autobuslinie
Autobuslijn Eindpunt
Capolinea Autobus
Terminus de Linea Autobus

34

PUBLIC HOUSE
Pub
Ausschank
Herberg
Taverna
Taberna

The Spaniards ★ Inn

TOILET Toilette Toilet Toeletta Retrete WC

BIKE STAND La Station Vélo Bike Station
Bicicletta stazione La estación bicicletas ⊖

BARCLAYS CYCLE HIRE - for short journeys Bike Stands are positioned approx. 300 metres apart. The **Access Fee** is £2 for a 24 hour period - return it inside 30 minutes and you will not pay the Usage Charge............**be careful - you must wait for at least 5 minutes between each trip!** The **Usage Payment** or the Hiring Payment is by Debit or Credit Card online or at the docking station.

The **Usage Charge / 30 minutes are free:**
1 Hour.............£1	2½ Hours...........£10	24 Hours.............£50.
1½ Hours.........£4	4 Hours.............£15	
2 Hours.............£6	6 Hours.............£35	

WHEN HIRING ALWAYS CHECK YOUR TYRES.
HIRING BEGINS WHEN THE KEY IS IN THE DOCKING POINT.
AT THE END OF A TRIP MAKE SURE WHEN YOU DOCK THE CYCLE - THE GREEN LIGHT GOES ON, OTHERWISE YOU WILL CONTINUE BEING CHARGED!

CHECK THIS INTERNET SITE FOR YOUR NEAREST BARCLAYS CYCLE STAND AND READ VERY CAREFULLY THE INSTRUCTIONS
http://www.//www.tfl.gov.uk/roadusers/cycling/14811.aspx

UNDERGROUND SYSTEM

MARBLE ARCH 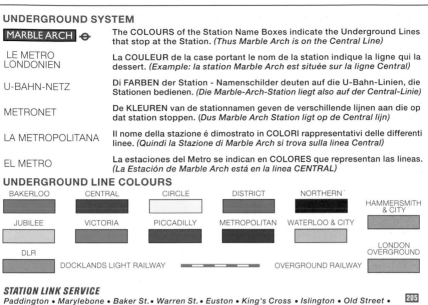 The COLOURS of the Station Name Boxes indicate the Underground Lines that stop at the Station. *(Thus Marble Arch is on the Central Line)*

LE METRO LONDONIEN — La COULEUR de la case portant le nom de la station indique la ligne qui la dessert. *(Example: la station Marble Arch est située sur la ligne Central)*

U-BAHN-NETZ — Di FARBEN der Station - Namenschilder deuten auf die U-Bahn-Linien, die Stationen bedienen. *(Die Marble-Arch-Station liegt also auf der Central-Linie)*

METRONET — De KLEUREN van de stationnamen geven de verschillende lijnen aan die op dat station stoppen. *(Dus Marble Arch Station ligt op de Central lijn)*

LA METROPOLITANA — Il nome della stazione é dimostrato in COLORI rappresentativi delle differenti linee. *(Quindi la Stazione di Marble Arch si trova sulla linea Central)*

EL METRO — La estaciones del Metro se indican en COLORES que representan las lineas. *(La Estación de Marble Arch está en la linea CENTRAL)*

UNDERGROUND LINE COLOURS

BAKERLOO	CENTRAL	CIRCLE	DISTRICT	NORTHERN

HAMMERSMITH & CITY

JUBILEE	VICTORIA	PICCADILLY	METROPOLITAN	WATERLOO & CITY

LONDON OVERGROUND

DLR — DOCKLANDS LIGHT RAILWAY — OVERGROUND RAILWAY

STATION LINK SERVICE
Paddington • Marylebone • Baker St.• Warren St.• Euston • King's Cross • Islington • Old Street • Moorgate • Liverpool St.• Aldgate • Whitechapel Road • Whitechapel • Mile End • Bow Church   **205**

DAY BUS ROUTES WITH NUMBERS
Ligne d'autobus quotidienne avec numéros - Busstrecke tagsüber mit linien-nummern
Dagelijkse Autobuslijn met Nummers - Autobus quotidiano con Numeri
La Ruta de Autobuses durante día con Números

BUS ROUTES in GREY
Arrows indicate BUSES in one direction only.
Lignes d'autobus en GRIS. *Les flèches indiquent les lignes d'autobus dans un seul sens.*
GRAUE busstrecken.
Pfeile zeigen auf Busverkehr nur in Pfeil-richtung.
Autobuslijnen in GRIJS.
Pijlen geven de bussen aan in één richting.
Linee di Autobus in GRIGIO.
Le frecce indicano autobus in una sola direzione.
Ruta autobús en GRIS.
Las flechas indican la ruta de los autobuses en una sola dirección.

42 78

BUS ROUTE NUMBERS are indicated in the border.
Les lignes dépassant les bordures de la carte sont indiquées en marge.
Buslinien-Nummern sind am Kartenrand angegeben.
Bus route nummers zijn aangegeven in de kantlijn.
I numeri delle linee di autobus son indicate sul margine.
Los números de autobús se indican en el margen.

PLACES OF INTEREST - ENDROITS INTERESSANTS - SEHENSWÜRDIGKEITEN - BEZIENSWAARDIGHEDEN - LUOGHI DI INTERESSE - LUGARES DE INTERES

IMPORTANT BUILDINGS
Bâtiments importants
Wichtige Gebäude
Belangrijke gebouwen
Edifici importanti
Edifícios importantes

BANK OF ENGLAND

BUILDINGS open to the PUBLIC
Edifices ouverts au public
Allgemein zugängliche Gebäude
Gebouwen met toegang voor het publiek
Edifici aperti al pubblico
Edificios abiertos al público

ST.PAUL'S CATHEDRAL

SHOPPING - MAGASINS - EINKÄUFE - WINKELEN - ACQUISTI - COMPRAS

A SELECTION OF SHOPS - Choix de Magasins - Einige Läden - Keus van Winkels - Scelta di Negozi - Selección de Tiendas

LIBERTY

STREET MARKETS - Marché en plein air - Straßenmarkt - Straatmarkt
Mercato all'aperto - Mercado callejero

M

TICKETS The TRAVEL CARD available for 1-3-7 days is the easy way to travel on the Tube, Buses, or Docklands Rail - it also gives 33% discount on River Services. The Central Zones 1-2 are probably all you will need: tickets can be obtained at Tube Stations or Tourist Offices. Note you can use a 1-2 zone ticket in all 6 zones on London Transport Buses.

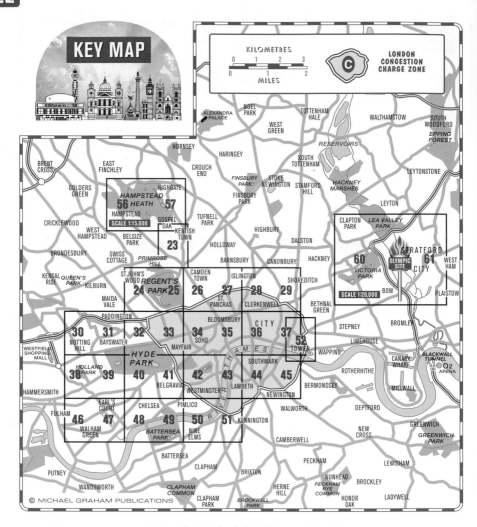

KEY MAP

KILOMETRES
0 1 2 3

MILES
0 1 2

C

LONDON
CONGESTION
CHARGE ZONE

ALEXANDRA PALACE
NOEL PARK
TOTTENHAM HALE
WALTHAMSTOW
SOUTH WOODFORD
WEST GREEN
EPPING FOREST
HORNSEY
HARINGEY
RESERVOIRS
BRENT CROSS
EAST FINCHLEY
CROUCH END
SOUTH TOTTENHAM
LEYTONSTONE
GOLDERS GREEN
HIGHGATE
FINSBURY PARK
STOKE NEWINGTON
STAMFORD HILL
HACKNEY MARSHES
LEYTON
CRICKLEWOOD
56 HAMPSTEAD HEATH **57**
HAMPSTEAD
SCALE 1:15,000
TUFNELL PARK
CLAPTON PARK
LEA VALLEY PARK
WEST HAMPSTEAD
GOSPEL OAK
KENTISH TOWN
HIGHBURY
STRATFORD
BRONDESBURY
BELSIZE PARK
23
HOLLOWAY
DALSTON
OLYMPIC SITE
61 WEST HAM
SWISS COTTAGE
PRIMROSE HILL
BARNSBURY
CANONBURY
HACKNEY
60 VICTORIA PARK
61 CITY
KENSAL RISE
QUEEN'S PARK
KILBURN
ST JOHN'S WOOD
24 REGENT'S PARK **25**
CAMDEN TOWN
ISLINGTON
SHOREDITCH
SCALE 1:20,000
BOW
PLAISTOW
MAIDA VALE
26
27
28
29
ST. PANCRAS
CLERKENWELL
BETHNAL GREEN
PADDINGTON
BLOOMSBURY
CITY
STEPNEY
BROMLEY
30 NOTTING HILL
31 BAYSWATER
32
33
34 SOHO
35
36
37 **52** TOWER
LIMEHOUSE
WAPPING
CANARY WHARF
BLACKWALL TUNNEL
Q2 ARENA
WESTFIELD SHOPPING MALL
HYDE PARK
MAYFAIR
SOUTHWARK
ROTHERHITHE
MILLWALL
HOLLAND PARK
38
39
40
41
42
43
44
45
BELGRAVIA
WESTMINSTER
LAMBETH
BERMONDSEY
HAMMERSMITH
NEWINGTON
WALWORTH
DEPTFORD
GREENWICH
FULHAM
EARL'S COURT
CHELSEA
PIMLICO
46
47
48
49
50
51 KENNINGTON
NEW CROSS
GREENWICH PARK
WALHAM GREEN
BATTERSEA PARK
NINE ELMS
CAMBERWELL
BATTERSEA
PECKHAM
LEWISHAM
PUTNEY
CLAPHAM
BRIXTON
NUNHEAD
BROCKLEY
WANDSWORTH
CLAPHAM COMMON
HERNE HILL
PECKHAM RYE COMMON
HONOR OAK
LADYWELL
CLAPHAM PARK
BROCKWELL PARK

© MICHAEL GRAHAM PUBLICATIONS

SCALE

approximately 6 inches to 1 mile
1 CENTIMETRE TO 100 METRES

1:10,000

300 METRES EQUAL 328 YARDS

METRES

0   100   200   300

🇬🇧 **ENGLISH** The maps are divided into 300 metre squares with divisions of 100 metres indicated in the border.

🇫🇷 **FRANÇAIS** Les cartes sont divisées en carrés de 300 mètres de côté, avec divisions de 100 mètres indiquées en bordure.

🇩🇪 **DEUTSCH** Die karten sind in karrees von 300 quadratmeter unterteilt 100-Meter-Unterteilung ist am Rand markiert.

NEDERLANDS De kaarten zijn verdeeld in vierkanten van 300 meter met verdelingen van 100 meter in de kantlijn.

🇮🇹 **ITALIANO** Le mappe sono suddivise in 300 metri quadrati con divisione di 100 metri indicate nel margine.

🇪🇸 **ESPAÑOL** Las cartas están divididas en cuadrados de 300 metros, con divisiones de 100 metros indicados en el margen.

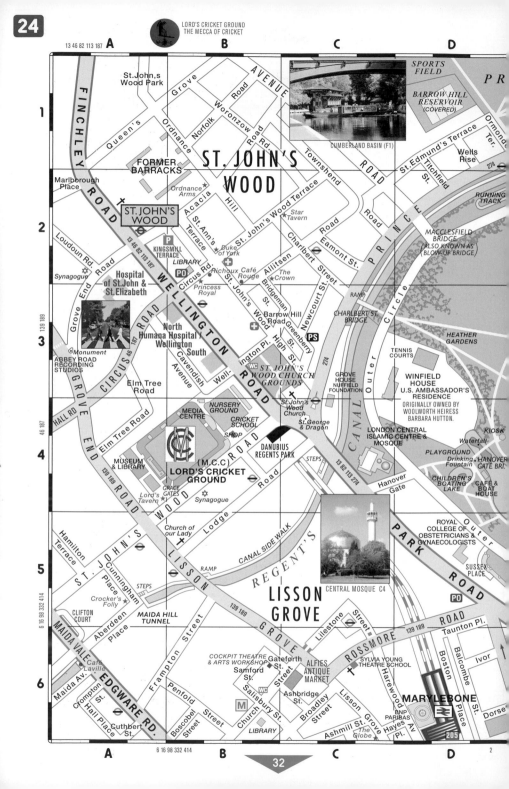

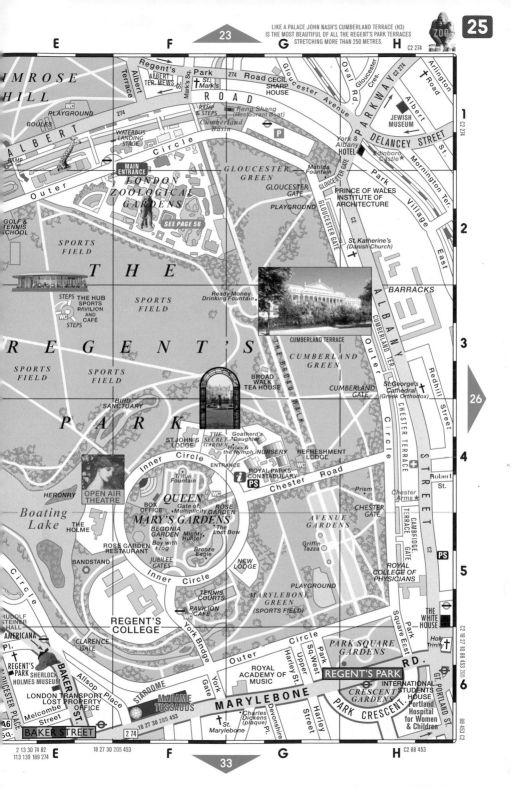

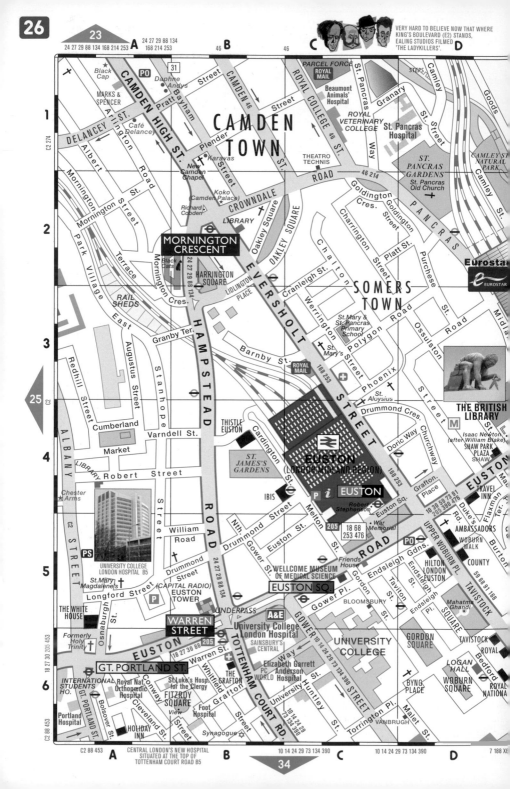

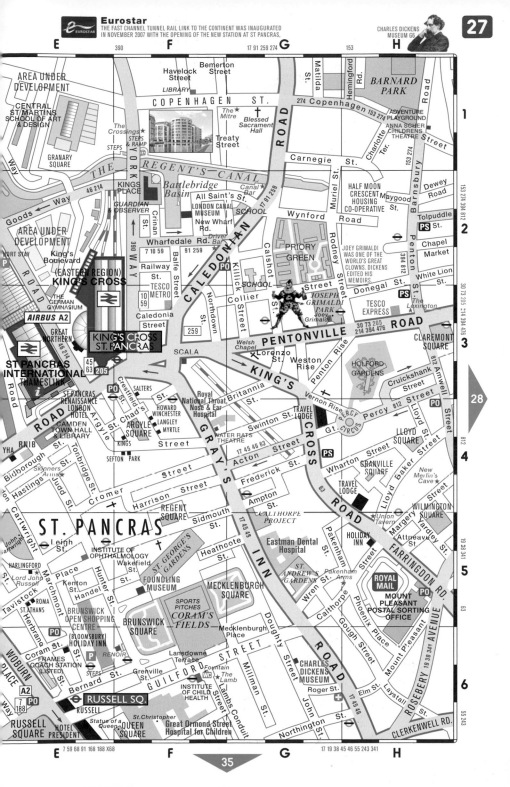

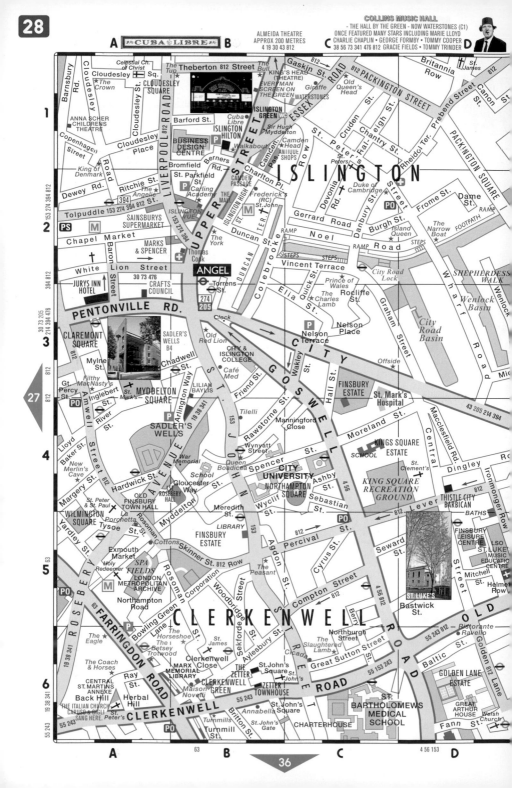

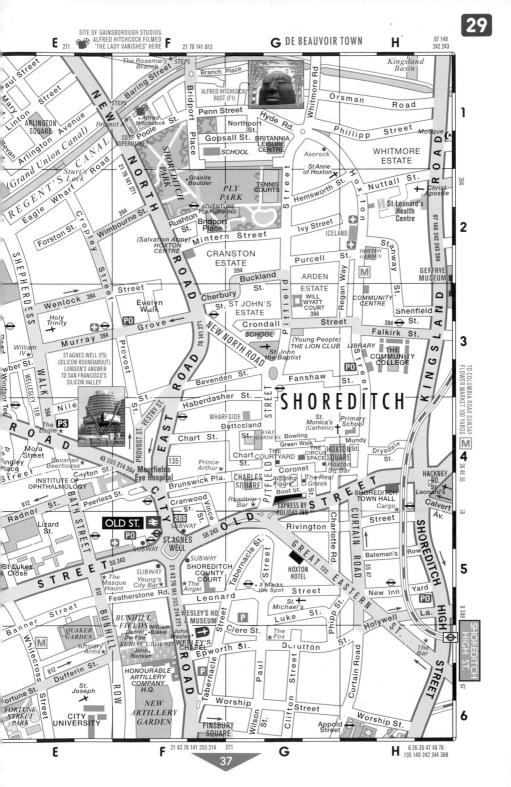

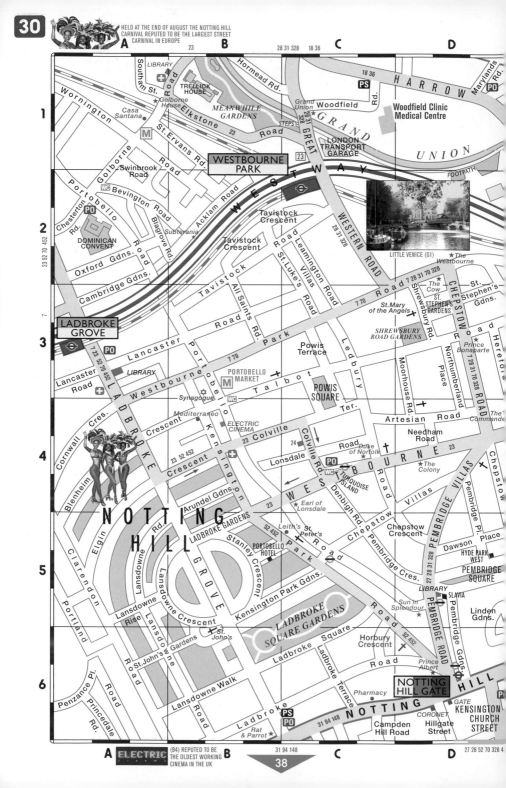

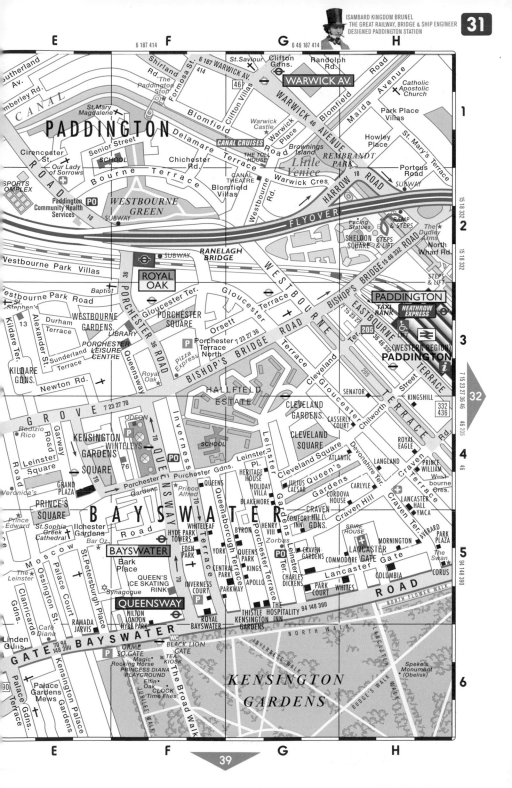

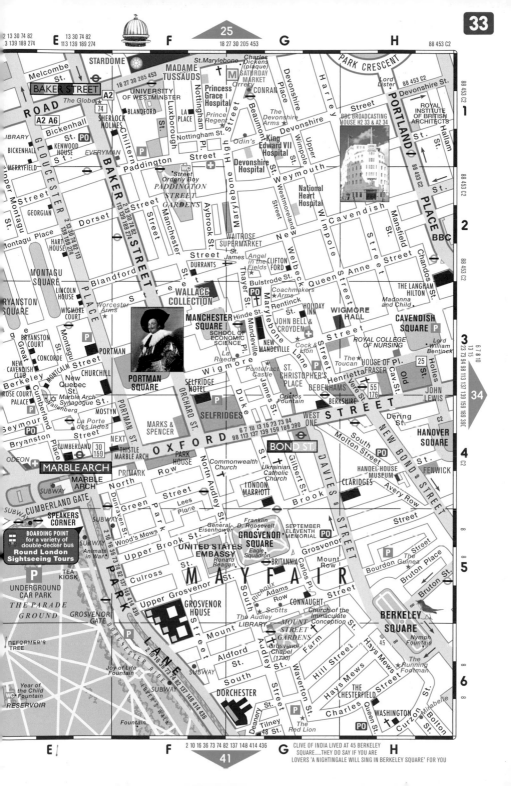

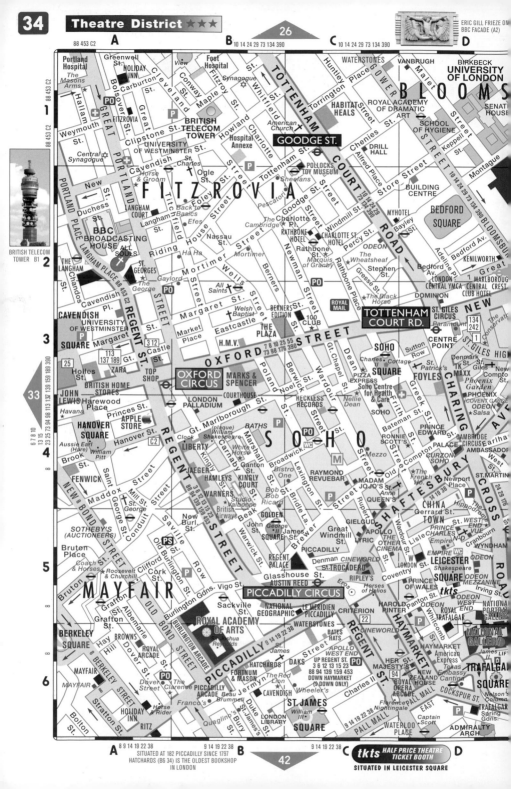

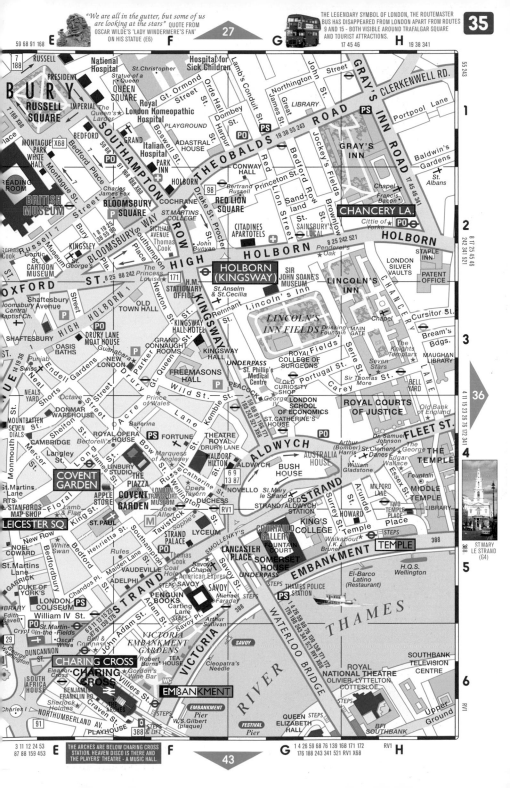

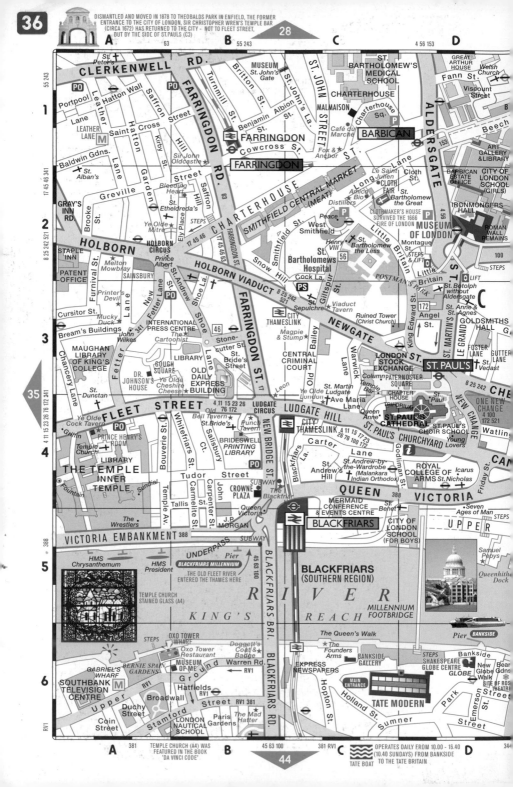

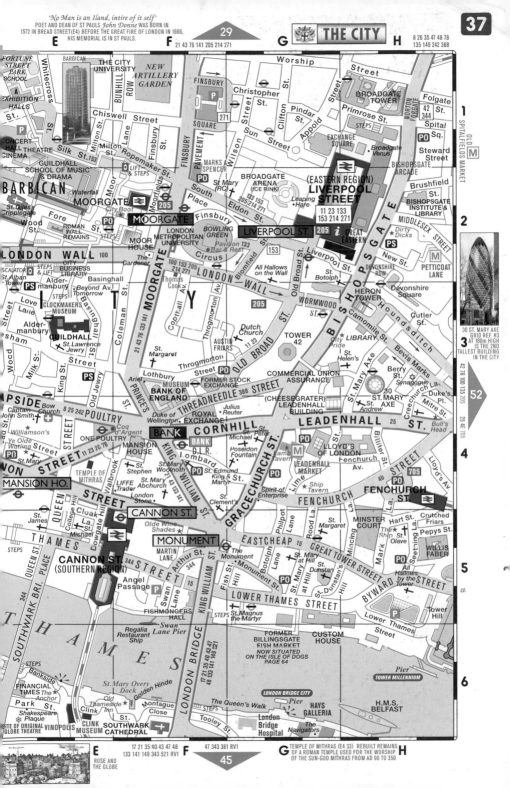

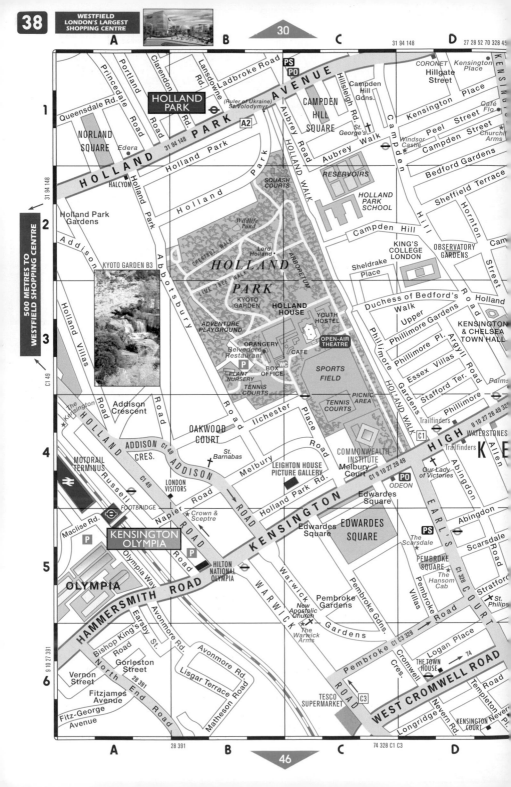

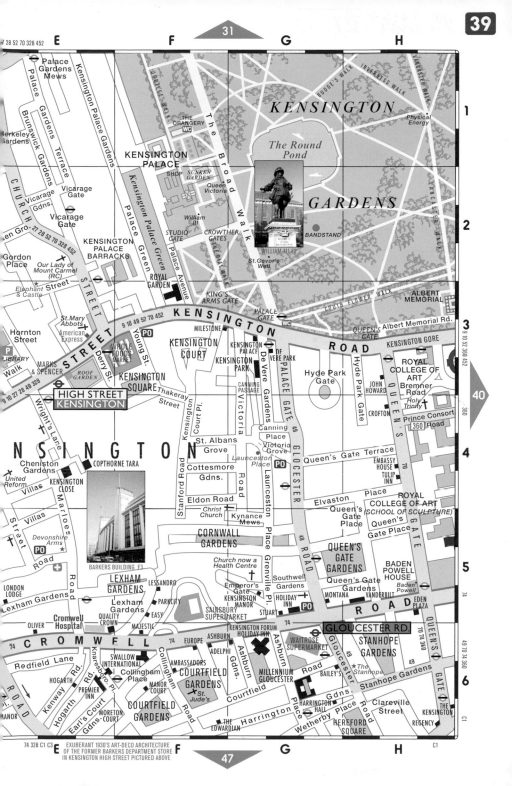

EXUBERANT 1930'S ART-DECO ARCHITECTURE OF THE FORMER BARKERS DEPARTMENT STORE IN KENSINGTON HIGH STREET PICTURED ABOVE

ADORNED WITH A FIG LEAF THE 18-FOOT-HIGH STATUE OF ACHILLES WAS CAST FROM CANNONS CAPTURED BY THE DUKE OF WELLINGTON; IT WAS A TRIBUTE TO THE DUKE FUNDED FROM SUBSCRIPTION BY 'LADIES OF QUALITY'

IN GREEN PARK (H2) STANDS THE MEMORIAL TO OVER 55,000 BOMBER COMMAND AIRCREW WHO LOST THEIR LIVES IN WORLD WAR 2.

WELLINGTON ARCH

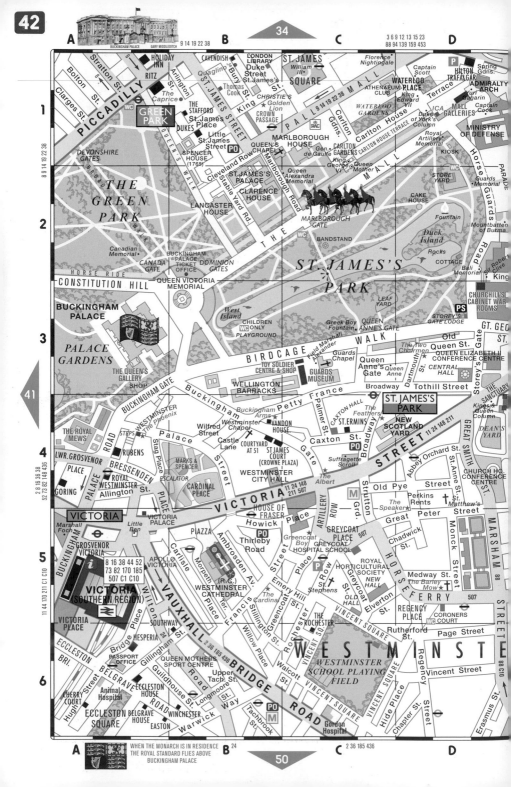

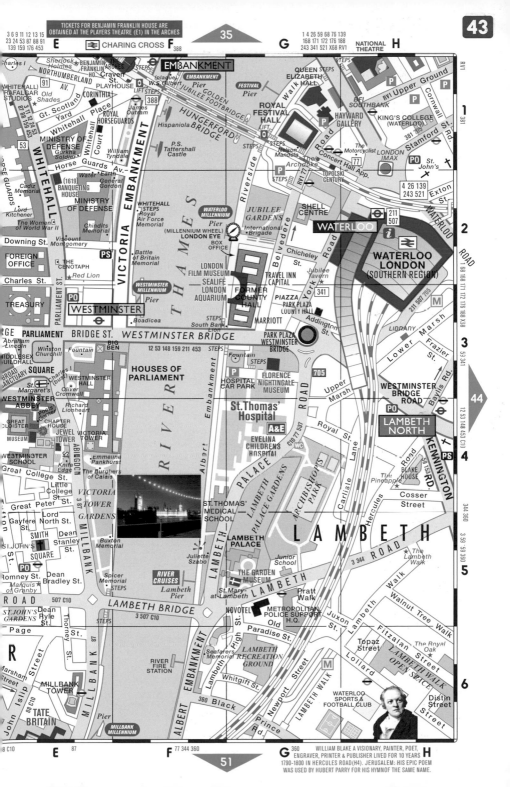

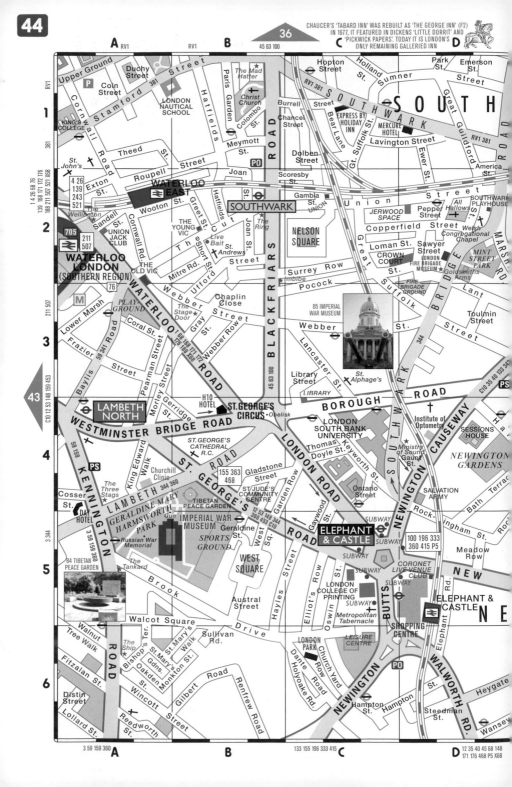

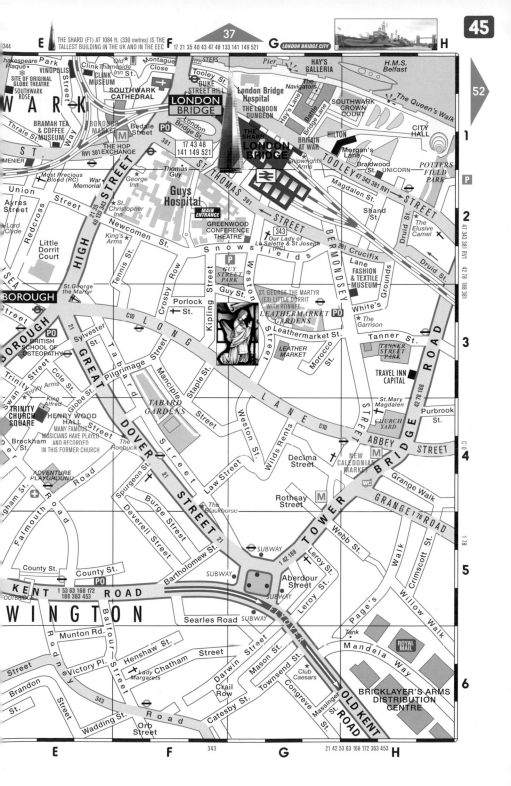

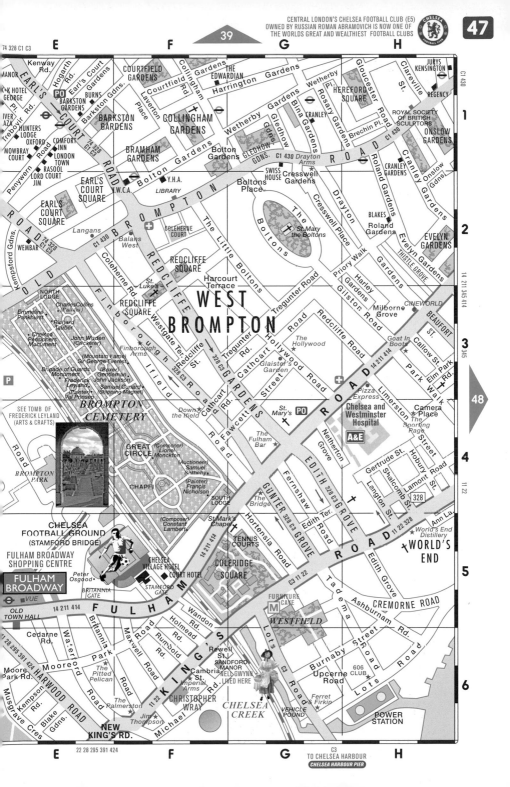

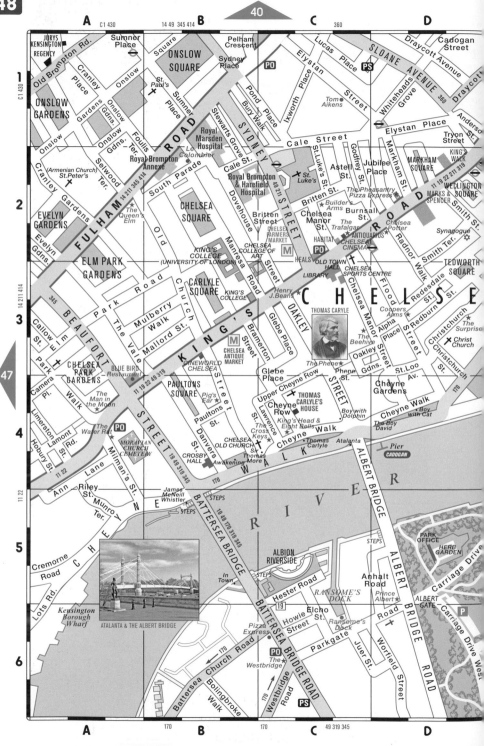

ATALANTA & THE ALBERT BRIDGE

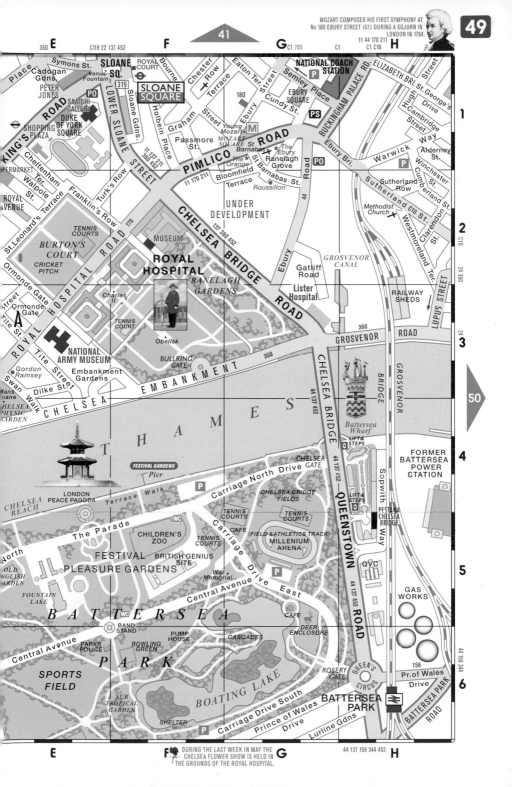

MOZART COMPOSED HIS FIRST SYMPHONY AT No 180 EBURY STREET (G1) DURING A SOJURN IN LONDON IN 1764.

DURING THE LAST WEEK IN MAY THE CHELSEA FLOWER SHOW IS HELD IN THE GROUNDS OF THE ROYAL HOSPITAL.

THE UNITED STATES EMBASSY IN GROSVENOR SQUARE
IS DUE TO RELOCATE TO A SITE CLOSE BY TO THE
RIVER THAMES AT NINE ELMS IN THE FUTURE

A 24 B 42 2 36 185 436 C D 88 C

42
2 36 185 436
49

1

Hugh St.
ECCLESTON SQUARE
BELGRAVE HOUSE
EASTON
HAMILTON HOUSE
WINCHESTER Way
BELGRAVE
SAINT GEORGE'S
Warwick St.
ECCLESTON SQUARE
The Country Pub in London
HANOVER
WARWICK SQUARE
CASWELL
St. Gabriel's
Cambridge St.
Alderney St.
Warwick St.
Churton St.
Villa Medici
Charlwood St.
Denbigh St.
St.
Tachbrook St.
VICTORIA
St.James the Less
Gordon Hospital
VINCENT SQUARE
VAUXHALL BRIDGE ROAD
Hide Pl.
Chapter St.
Douglas Street
Regency Street
Causton St.
St. Dominic's
2 36 185 436
Erasmus St.
MILLBANK GARDENS
Herrick St.
White Swan
Cureton St.
Ponsonby
JOHN ISL
PIMLICO
BESSBOROUGH GDNS

2

Cumberland St.
Clarendon St.
OXFORD HOUSE
Winchester Street
Sutherland St.
Sussex St.
Westmoreland Ter.
The Contented Vine
LUPUS STREET
Gloucester St.
DRIVE
St. Charlwood
Denbigh St.
PIMLICO
STREET
CLAVERTON STREET
St. Saviour's
Chichester St.
Rhodes on the Square
ST.GEORGE'S SQUARE
Moreton Place
Moreton St.
BESSBOROUGH ST.
PIMLICO LIBRARY
Bessborough Place
Aylesford St.
Fountain
ROAD

3

LUPUS STREET
LIBRARY
PO
CHURCHILL GARDENS ESTATE
Churchill Gardens Road
All Saints
GROSVENOR
Johnson's Place
DOLPHIN SQUARE
Villa de Cesari
WESTMINSTER BOATING BASE
The Helmsman
Statue
PIMLICO GARDENS
RIVER THA

←H4 49
CHELSEA BRIDGE WHARF

49

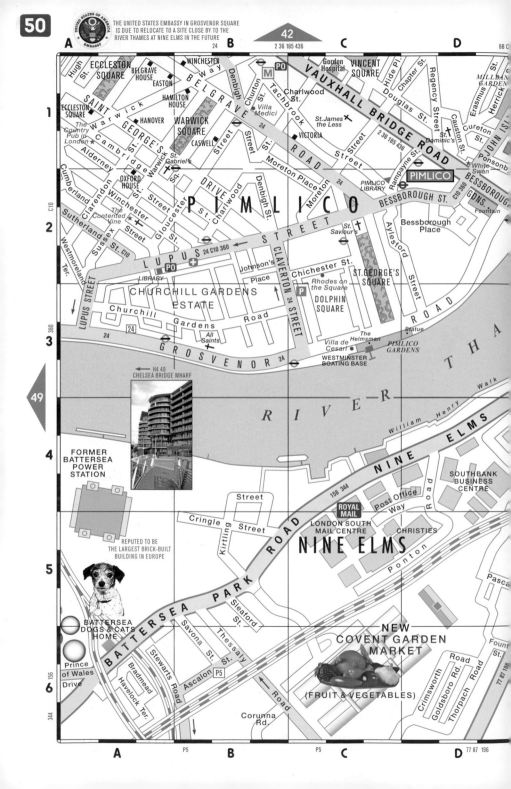

4

FORMER BATTERSEA POWER STATION

REPUTED TO BE THE LARGEST BRICK-BUILT BUILDING IN EUROPE

R I V E R   T H A M E S

NINE ELMS
William Henry Walk
SOUTHBANK BUSINESS CENTRE

5

Cringle Street
Kirtling Street
BATTERSEA PARK ROAD
NINE ELMS
ROYAL MAIL
LONDON SOUTH MAIL CENTRE
Post Office Way
Ponton Road
CHRISTIES
156 344
Pasca

BATTERSEA DOGS & CATS HOME
Prince of Wales Drive

6

Bradmead
Havelock Ter.
Stewarts Road
Savona St.
Ascalon St.
Thessaly Rd.
Sleaford St.
P5
PARK ROAD
Corunna Rd.
NEW COVENT GARDEN MARKET
(FRUIT & VEGETABLES)
Crimsworth Road
Goldsboro Rd.
Thorpach Road
Fount St.
77 87 196

A P5 B P5 C D 77 87 196

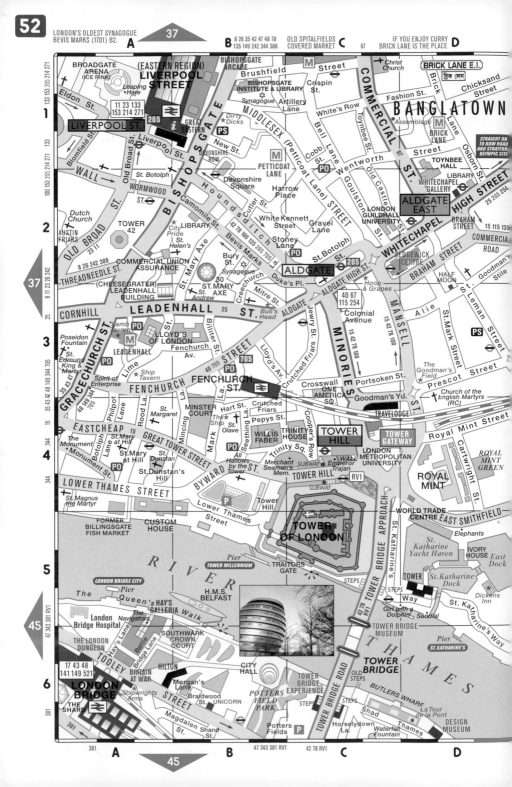

53

THE TOWER OF LONDON

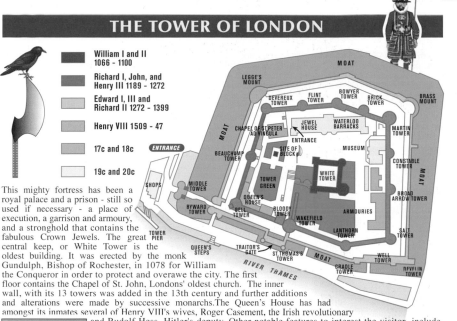

William I and II
1066 - 1100

Richard I, John, and
Henry III 1189 - 1272

Edward I, III and
Richard II 1272 - 1399

Henry VIII 1509 - 47

17c and 18c — ENTRANCE

19c and 20c

This mighty fortress has been a royal palace and a prison - still so used if necessary - a place of execution, a garrison and armoury, and a stronghold that contains the fabulous Crown Jewels. The great central keep, or White Tower is the oldest building. It was erected by the monk Gundulph, Bishop of Rochester, in 1078 for William the Conqueror in order to protect and overawe the city. The first floor contains the Chapel of St. John, Londons' oldest church. The inner wall, with its 13 towers was added in the 13th century and further additions and alterations were made by successive monarchs.The Queen's House has had amongst its inmates several of Henry VIII's wives, Roger Casement, the Irish revolutionary and Rudolf Hess, Hitler's deputy. Other notable features to interest the visitor include the Bloody Tower, with its portcullis, where Sir Walter Raleigh began to write his unfinished "History of the World", Traitors' Gate through which state prisoners passed, the Jewel House with the Crown Jewels and the White Tower which contains a wonderful collection of arms and armour - look for HenryVIII's armour for an idea of his real size. On Tower Green is the site of the execution block and the tower ravens. Always here are the Yeoman Warders - Beefeaters - in their traditional uniform.

THE NORMAN Tuesday - Saturday 9.00 - 17.30 Charge *If you book on line it is cheaper*
WHITE TOWER Sunday - Monday 10.00 - 17.30 *www.hrp.org.uk*

RIVER AND CANAL TRIPS

RIVER TRIPS Splendid trips are available on the River Thames during the summer months. In the evenings there are also supper trips for that special family or romantic occasion. These regular boat services run the whole length of the river, from April to October, when they revert to winter schedules. Within the London area there are daily services from Westminster Bridge, upriver to Kew Gardens, Hampton Court, and the riverside at Richmond, and downriver to the Tower of London, Greenwich and the Thames Barrier. Supper cruises also embark from Westminster Pier.
From Charing Cross Pier there are services to and from Tower Bridge and Greenwich.
From the rail terminals at Waterloo and Paddington there are combined Rail-River trips going to and from Windsor, Staines, Maidenhead, Marlow, Oxford and other attractive places along the river.
Full information on these trips is available from
Charing Cross Pier (map ref. F6 35) ☎ 7987 1185
Westminster Pier (F3 43) ☎ 7930 9033
Visit London ☎ 0870 1566 366

THE THAMES BARRIER This remarkable piece of engineering is the world's largest moveable defense against flooding. Cruises to the flood barrier embark from Westminster Pier and Lambeth Pier stopping at Canary Wharf and Greenwich. ☎ 7930 3373

CANAL TRIPS Frequent waterbus services run on the Regent's Canal by the London Waterbus Company starting from Little Venice, Paddington (G1 31), passing through Regent's Park to the London Zoo.
Inclusive Waterbus and Zoo tickets can be bought.
There are also narrow boat cruises from Blomfield Road (Little Venice) to Camden Lock and from Camden Lock to the Zoo and Little Venice.
London Waterbus Company
Camden Lock, NW1 ☎ 7482 2550
Jason's Trip runs from Little Venice to Camden Lock in an original painted narrow boat along the Grand Union Canal and the Regent's Canal.
Restaurant. Snacks, beer, wine, soft drinks on sale.
Booking Office ☎ 7286 3428
There are "Jenny Wren" cruises on the Regent's Canal in traditionally decorated narrow boats through the Zoo, Regent's Park and Maida Hill tunnel.
250 Camden High Street,NW1 ☎ 7485 4433
The "Fair Lady" narrow boat has a restaurant and runs dinner cruises from Tuesday to Saturday 19.30 or 20.00 hours, and lunch cruises on Sundays 12.30 or 13.00 hours but booking in advance for these is essential at Camden Lock Office.
277 Camden High Street, NW1 ☎ 7485 6210

PLACES OF INTEREST AROUND LONDON

HAMPTON COURT PALACE   Until 1514 a fine country mansion stood on this site in its lovely situation twelve miles down river from Westminster. Then the ascending (at that time) Cardinal Thomas Wolsey acquired the land and the house and began building this elegant and stately palace. When he fell from favour with his royal master Henry VIII he tried to stave off his inevitable downfall by presenting the palace in 1528 to the King - all to no avail, Wolsey died the next year. Henry really enjoyed the palace and moved in with his mistress and "owne darling", Anne Boleyn. He continued sumptuously enlarging the palace: the grounds, the vast kitchens with their huge fireplaces, and he also added tennis courts. Possibly two of the best parts of the original Tudor building commissioned by Henry are the beamed *Great Hall* with its magnificent tapestries and stained-glass windows, and the *Clock Court* which contains the famous *Astronomical Clock* (1540)which was originally in Henry's other palace in St James.

When William and Mary jointly came to the throne in 1689 there were plans afoot to demolish the palace, but fortunately they employed Sir Christopher Wren to enclose the south front and entirely rebuild the east side; within which he created the beautiful cloistered *Fountain Court*. During William's reign *The Maze*, a circular version, was created, later it was replaced by the triangular maze in 1715.

The house has many great paintings and however time-limited you are it is well worth a visit. A noble feature of the gardens is the most famous vine in the world, the vigorous black hamburg grapevine *The Great Vine* planted in 1768 by Capability Brown.

Approached by rail (within Zone 6 if you have a travel card) from Waterloo Station to Hampton Court then a 200 metre walk over the bridge. Perhaps the most interesting approach is by riverboat from Westminster - it can take about 4 hours.
The Gardens are open to the public daily until dusk except Christmas Day.
Palace and Maze *Winter November - March Monday to Sunday 10.00 - 16.30.*
Summer April - October 10.00 - 18.00 Closed 24th to the 26th December

BUSHY PARK Across Hampton Court Road lies this 1100-acre former hunting park still containing over 300 deer. Near the Hampton Court gate you will see the *Diana Fountain* (1713) and beyond for one mile *Chestnut Avenue*, a vista to behold in spring. During WW2 Bushy was the US 8th Army headquarters for Operation Overlord in 1944, with General Eisenhower, supreme commander.

HENRY VIII BY HANS HOLBEIN

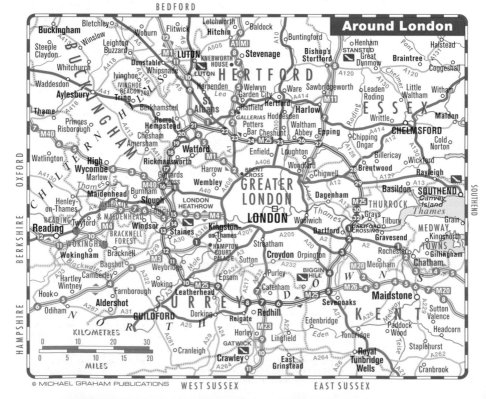

© MICHAEL GRAHAM PUBLICATIONS

HATFIELD HOUSE and BISHOP'S PALACE
Main Gate situated opposite Hatfield Station.   Acquired by Henry VIII after the Dissolution, the old Palace built in 1485 became a home for his children. Later Elizabeth I was confined to the palace by her sister Mary Tudor who was at that time Queen. The splendid Jacobean house was built by Robert Cecil, the first Earl of Salisbury, between 1607-12, he had exchanged with James I, Theobalds Park for the Palace. All that remains of the Palace is one wing, which was made into stables, and is now used as a restaurant with occasional Elizabethan banquets. The house has many fine paintings, furniture, armour, tapestries and relics dating back to the 15th century. The Marble Hall which takes up the width of the Jacobean house contains two paintings of Elizabeth I, both are exquisite. On the Grand Staircase there is a painting of a horse which is reputed to have been ridden by Elizabeth to review her troops before the Spanish Armada. Elizabeth's gardening hat, gloves and silk stockings will no doubt interest followers of fashion. The gardens are worth a visit in their own right to see the work of the famous 17th century gardening botanists - father and son, both named John Tradescant. A Festival of Gardening is held on the third weekend in June.

RAINBOW PORTRAIT OF ELIZABETH I BY ISAAC OLIVER (1565-1617)

Easter Saturday - 30th September 12.00 - 17.00,
Wednesday to Sunday and Bank Holidays.   *Charge*

KEW GARDENS A lovely 300-acre park and arboretum adjacent to the River Thames, ten miles from Central London with stately tree-lined avenues and sequestered walks. The many features to peruse include: a *Chinese Pagoda* (164 foot high), a *Japanese Gateway (*a smaller version of a Buddhist Temple gate in Kyoto), Conservatories, a *Palm House*, an *Orangery*, and the latest addition a *Woodland Walk* 18 metres high, 200 metres long opened in 2008 - it safely moves and sways in the wind! Whether you go when the bluebells are out or the daffodils are blooming, any season holds unknown surprises - for me the glorious rhododenderon trees in bloom is always a good time to visit.

THE PALM HOUSE

Take the District Line tube to Kew Gardens Station then walk down Lichfield Road to the Victoria Gate entrance.
Open *Winter 9.30-16.15, except 24th-25th December, Summer 9.30-18.30, weekends 19.30. Children go free / Charge*

ST. ALBANS Steeped in history: a Celtic settlement *Verlamion* long before the Romans arrived and built their town and a theatre by the River Ver. In AD 61 it was set on fire by the warrior Queen Boudiccca. On the hill where the Abbey stands today, a Roman called Alban became the first Christian martyr to die in Britain.

It is difficult to believe, but underneath the rolling hills of *Verulamium Park* is another Pompeii. In the park there are several outcrops of the *Roman Wall* and a *Hypocaust* which shows you the underfloor heating system the Romans used. Across the way from the superb unmissable *Verulamium Museum* are the remains of the Roman theatre on the Gorhambury estate: a lovely walk takes you to the original ruined *Gorhambury House* where Sir Francis Bacon and his father before him lived. After the martyrdom of Alban, a Saxon church stood on the hill: parts of this church were incorporated into the transept of the Norman abbey which became the focal point of a large monastery. There is so much to relate concerning *St Albans Abbey*: the first draft of Magna Carta was read here, the ceiling of the central tower with red and white roses depicts the Church's ambiguous approach to the Wars of the Roses - the opening battle was fought in St. Albans.

At the bottom of the hill at the side of the River Ver is the *Fighting Cocks,* a 'Medieval Dovecote' built over a former monastery building in 1600 and recognised as the oldest

CLOCK TOWER ST ALBANS

inhabited public house in the country officially accepted and entered in the Guinness Book of Records. The name reflects one of its previous attractions. *St. Albans is 35 minutes from St Pancras on a fast train or try the* **uno** *bus 712 or 714 from Victoria Coach Station or Marble Arch which takes approximately 75 minutes.*   *Do check the Official Bus Time Tables*

ABBEY AND FIGHTING COCKS BY RONALD MADDOX

KNEBWORTH HOUSE
Accessed from the A1(M) Externally the palatial building is Victorian Gothic, the figment of author Edward Bulwer-Lytton's imagination. It is though much more than that. The magnificent Banqueting Hall partly dates from the Jacobean period and contains a 1930s painting by Winston Churchill of the hall; private theatricals were performed here by a group led by Charles Dickens. The Library contains many Lytton family treasures including a unique Dutch musical clock. The Lytton family had connections with India, and the British Raj exhibition, housed in a former squash court, contains many mementoes.
The features of the original gardens are gradually being restored and include a rose garden, sunken lawn and a maze. For the family there is a narrow gauge railway, adventure playground and picnic areas.
Knebworth is renowned for its medieval jousting tournaments, and concerts of great jazz, rock and pop artists during the summer months.   *Guided Tours of the House only.*
Open Daily from early April - end of September.   *Charge*

THE BANQUETING HALL, KNEBWORTH HOUSE   *Park, Gardens, Playground and Railway 11.00 -17.30 House & Indian Raj Display 12.00-17.00*

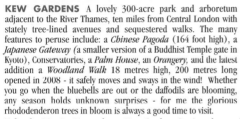

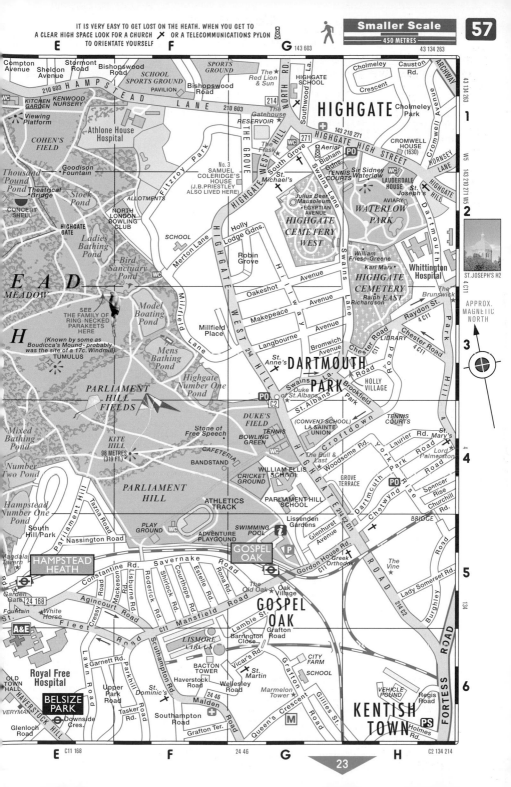

THE LONDON ZOO

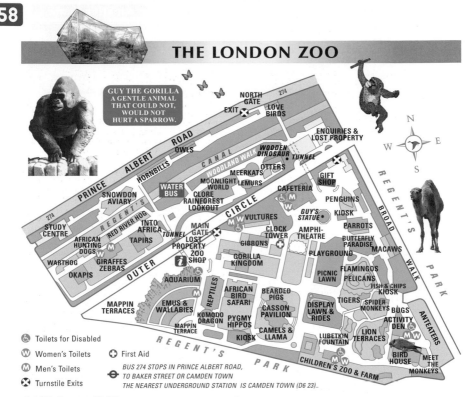

GUY THE GORILLA
A GENTLE ANIMAL
THAT COULD NOT,
WOULD NOT
HURT A SPARROW.

NORTH GATE 274
EXIT
LOVE BIRDS
ENQUIRIES & LOST PROPERTY
ALBERT ROAD
OWLS
WOODEN DINOSAUR
TUNNEL
HORNBILLS
CANAL
WOODLAND WALK
OTTERS
MEERKATS
GIFT SHOP
MOONLIGHT WORLD
LEMURS
CAFETERIA
PRINCE
SNOWDON AVIARY
WATER BUS
CLORE RAINFOREST LOOKOUT
PENGUINS
REGENT'S
RED RIVER HOG
CIRCLE
VULTURES
GUY'S STATUE
KIOSK
STUDY CENTRE
INTO AFRICA
MAIN GATE
CLOCK TOWER
AMPHI-THEATRE
PARROTS
AFRICAN HUNTING DOGS
TUNNEL
TAPIRS
LOST PROPERTY
GIBBONS
BUTTERFLY PARADISE
MACAWS
WARTHOG
GIRAFFES ZEBRAS
ZOO SHOP
GORILLA KINGDOM
PLAYGROUND
FLAMINGOS
OKAPIS
OUTER
AQUARIUM
REPTILES
PICNIC LAWN
PELICANS
FISH & CHIPS KIOSK
AFRICAN BIRD SAFARI
BEARDED PIGS
TIGERS
SPIDER MONKEYS
MAPPIN TERRACES
EMUS & WALLABIES
KOMODO DRAGON
CASSON PAVILION
DISPLAY LAWN & RIDES
BUGS
ACTIVITY DEN
MAPPIN TERRACE
PYGMY HIPPOS
CAMELS & LLAMA
LUBETKIN FOUNTAIN
LION TERRACES
REGENT'S
KIOSK
CHILDREN'S ZOO & FARM
BIRD HOUSE
MEET THE MONKEYS
PARK

REGENT'S BROAD WALK PARK ANTEATERS

🚻 Toilets for Disabled

Ⓦ Women's Toilets

Ⓜ Men's Toilets

✪ Turnstile Exits

✛ First Aid

BUS 274 STOPS IN PRINCE ALBERT ROAD, TO BAKER STREET OR CAMDEN TOWN

THE NEAREST UNDERGROUND STATION IS CAMDEN TOWN (D6 23)..

Grid Reference F2 25

The London Zoo is one of the oldest and most famous animal collections in the world, and, together with Whipsnade Park in Bedfordshire, forms part of the Zoological Society of London, a scientific society founded by Sir Stamford Raffles and others in 1826. The zoo extends over an area of 36 acres in Regent's Park. More than 12,000 animals live here, including lions, giraffes, gorillas, and many other species of mammals together with birds, reptiles, amphibians, fishes and insects. A high proportion of the animals were born here but many others come from other zoos throughout the world.

I loved this zoo as a child and still do try to visit London and Whipsnade twice a year. My father always had a particular fascination for the gentle gorillas and *Guy* in particular, who always gave you that quizzical look, weighing you up as much as you were him. Alas he is long gone, as is my father, but *Guy's* statue stands in the zoo and always jogs my memory of happy bygone days.

The Gorilla Kingdom is the lushly vegetated habitat for the west lowland gorillas, colobus monkeys, rainforest birds, and lizards; while the new Clore Rainforest Lookout has tropical trees, monkeys, birds, tiny tamarins, marmosets, and iguanas etc.

The hot-pool in the Casson Pavilion is where the pygmy hippos reside in winter: the building also houses camels and llamas. On the Mappin Terraces are emus and wallabies; underneath these terraces is the Aquarium which stretches for 150 yards, (Britains largest), with fishes from fresh, sea, and tropical waters all over the world. Seawater in the circulation system is topped up annually when it is brought in by road-tanker from the North Sea. Here you find deadly piranha fish with razor-sharp teeth, gently drifting seahorses, poisonous dragon fish, eels; all major groups of reptiles are represented - turtles

and terrapins, tortoises, crocodiles and alligators, brilliant coloured and camouflaged lizards, and snakes from the venomous to the benign, with vipers, pythons and boa constrictors.

Animal feeding times are staggered throughout the day and many visitors like to plan their passage through the zoo taking account of these times. Check the timetable when you enter the zoo.

The penguins always look important and are a favourite to watch. I like the way they move along in a queue-like procession, as though waiting for the bus back to Antarctica. They no longer inhabit the Lubetkin pool; this listed architectural delight, with spiral interlocking ramps was designed back in the 1930's by Berthold Lubetkin, today it has a featured fountain. The present penguin habitat is without a concrete base, so it is less toil on their feet!

A marvellous improvement are the Lion Terraces, the cats now live in open areas, rich with plants and grasses that reflect their natural habitat. Inside the Bird House are many beautiful species, including brilliant coloured parakeets, big beaked toucans and hornbills. The largest birds in the world (ostriches and storks) are found in the African Bird Safari enclosure. Guaranteed to make you shudder, the BUGS House contains great colonies of ants, praying mantises, stick insects, spiders and scorpions.

A particularly fascinating collection of creatures is assembled in the Moonlight World where assimilated 'night' is created to encourage nocturnal animals to become active in normal daytime. There are badgers, bush babies, flying foxes, lorises and douroucouli, the only nocturnal monkey in the world.

Open daily except Christmas Day.
Summer 10.00 - 17.30 April - September.
Winter 10.00 - 16.00.   *Charge*

LONDON'S PARKS AND VILLAGES

London is made especially beautiful by the wealth of its green open spaces, and its majestic squares that break the monotony of the grey buildings with their lovely flower-filled gardens. The largest and principal London parks are the Royal Parks, which are Crown property and are open to the public free.

The Royal Parks

THE GREEN PARK Located between Piccadilly and Constitution Hill, this is a relaxing park that is full of mature trees and grassland.

HYDE PARK With the adjoining Kensington Gardens, the park extends to 600 acres of grassland, trees and flower beds, with the Serpentine Lake for boating and fishing (only with a permit), and at the Lido, bathing. restaurants, band concerts, horse riding in Rotten Row, football, bowling and putting.

KENSINGTON GARDENS A former hunting ground laid out by William III, adjoining the west side of Hyde Park and creating a complete contrast - it is a more pleasant and peaceful place. There are Italian Gardens, the Round Pond for model boating, Long Water, the Peter Pan statue and the Albert Memorial.

PRIMROSE HILL From the summit of this grassy hill which is 68 metres (206ft) above sea level, there is a superb panorama of London. An engraved plaque identifies the buildings for you.

REGENT'S PARK A truly lovely park, framed by the beautiful terraced architecture of John Nash who designed this park at the request of the Prince Regent (later George IV). A rose garden, magnificent shrubs and trees, lawns, fountains, rowing on the lake, band concerts, the magical Open-Air Theatre and the Zoo are all part of this great park.

ST. JAMES'S PARK A one time deer park and now very beautiful with a picturesque bridge over an ornamental lake. Many wildfowl, pelicans and geese, fine views and band concerts.

Public Parks and Spaces

BATTERSEA PARK On the southside of the Thames, and the scene of the annual Easter parade. The Peace Pagoda (E5 49) was built in 1985 by Japanese monks to commemorate the tragic bombing of Hiroshima.

HAMPSTEAD HEATH They call the heath 'the lungs of London' and so it is. The heath is 792 acres of pure joy, great for flying kites, for walks through dells and uplands, for woods and unusual fauna. There are lakes for model boats, and swimming and fishing; animal enclosures and ornamental gardens: the Hill Garden (B3 56) with its pergola is well worth seeking out. On summer evenings Kenwood is a lovely setting for the open air Lakeside concerts from opera companies and symphony orchestras. I always enjoy a brisk walk over the heath with my wife after the excesses of Christmas.

HOLLAND PARK In the heart of Kensington and for the early part of the 20th century, a private garden. Includes a Japanese garden and an open air theatre.

WATERLOW PARK A favourite park of mine situated on top of Highgate Hill. Undulating, small and interesting at every turn, with recreational features, an aviary and Lauderdale House for musical events - classical and jazz.

> **THE ROOF GARDENS** In Kensington near Derry Street (E3 39) on the very top of a building that used to be occupied by Derry & Toms there is an absolutely magnificent and unique rooftop paradise garden; for two days (Thurs. & Sats.) a club and restaurant. Owned by Richard Branson, you can view this when there are no functions.

London's Villages

Before the 19th century and the expansion of the railways London was contained within the City, Westminster and Southwark. The communities that were outside these areas were villages. As transport extended, the villages became a part of the conurbation. Here are a few of the villages that are still discernible within the great conurbation.

HAMPSTEAD Page 56-57. When you arrive at Hampstead on the underground you are 64 metres below ground level in the deepest station in London, and on reaching the surface you know you are in a different atmosphere. For many years, Hampstead has been a haven for arts of all descriptions. John Constable who did many paintings of the heath is buried in the churchyard of St.John's (B5 56), as is John Harrison, the self-taught clockmaker who is attributed with defining 'Longitude' by means of his chronometer. The flagpole (B3 56) at the top of Heath Street is the highest point in London, although the best view is from the top of Parliament Hill. Legends of the highwayman, Dick Turpin, are rife in old pubs like *The Spaniards*, while many of the little back streets reveal surprising architecture mixed in with the cottages. There are numerous cafes and bistros and the fresh air on the heath is therapeutic.

Kenwood House * On the north side of the heath is this 17th century Robert Adam house, which has a fine collection of paintings, a Rembrandt self-portrait and works by Turner, Romney, Vermeer, Hals etc. The superb Adam Library is a feature worth looking out for. *Daily April - Sept 10.00 - 18.00 October - March 10.00 - 16.00* Free

HIGHGATE Page 57. Highgate has even more of a village atmosphere. Perched on the top of a hill, it deceptively seems higher than its near neighbour Hampstead. I have already mentioned Waterlow Park which is extremely pleasant, particularly during the week. The famous pub is *The Flask* (G1 57), which dates back to 1767.

On summer evenings the tables are filled with people enjoying the ale and food. John Betjeman loved the pub and they do say that Major Rogers, the frontiersman of 'Rogers Rangers' fame drank here - do you remember Spencer Tracy in the film *Northwest Passage?* Strangely, the biggest attraction in Highgate is the cemetery, for here Karl Marx was put to rest - his memorial is very striking and strong as though it was made forever. In the village there are many international restaurants.

ISLINGTON Page 28 . Home of many intellectuals and artists, not as ostentatious as Chelsea and always full of life. It has an antique shop mall and an antiques market; some great and famous fringe pub theatres like the *King's Head* (B1 28), where often a future West End or Broadway production can be seen in embryo form; the pub still rings your bar bill up in old shillings and pence! Islington is always enjoyable: there are many cafes and restaurants serving every cuisine imaginable: *Le Mercury*, the atmospheric *Cuba Libre* and Mexican *Desperados* (in its previous guise Tony Blair dined here) are all in Upper Street and serve excellent food that will not break your pocket; for more formal dining, *Frederick's* may suit you more. The Victorian pub, the *Camden Head*, has great atmosphere and good lunches (B1 28), and is also a comedy venue.

Kenwood House closed for refurbishment until 2013

DURING THE MID 18th CENTURY BOW WAS FAMOUS FOR QUALITY PORCELAIN MADE IN A FACTORY WHICH ONCE STOOD NEAR WHERE THE FLYOVER (F6) NOW STANDS. 200 EXAMPLES ARE IN THE VICTORIA AND ALBERT MUSEUM (B5 40).

THE FAMOUS MODEL MATCHBOX FACTORY STILL STANDS TODAY - CONVERTED INTO 'THE BOW QUARTER' APARTMENTS (E5 61) NEAR THE OLYMPIC STADIUM.

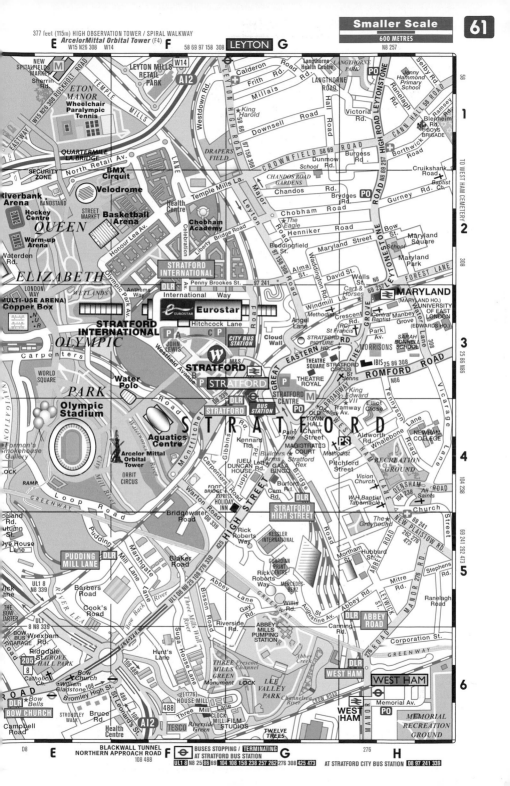

Just like the Lower East Side of New York, the East End of London was always a melting pot of cultures - people came from all over Europe seeking work and to improve their way of life. During the 16th and 17th centuries, Huguenots (Calvinist Protestants) fleeing from religious persecution arrived from France. Later in the 1780s many Chinese sailors working for the East India company docked in the Port of London (once the largest port in the world), they settled in Limehouse and worked in the docks. In the 20th century the area was often featured in films. I remember a musical with the song 'Limehouse Blues' danced to a backdrop of a foggy mysterious London inhabited by pig-tailed Chinese men and women smoking opium - the film was *Ziegfeld Follies* - in the scene Fred Astaire was a chinaman.

In 1740-41 the aftermath of the first Irish Famine brought large numbers of Irish men to the East End looking for work as labourers or dock-hands; their women went into the sweated labour garment trade or as domestic servants. A hundred years later the failure of the potato crop brought another famine to Ireland forcing more Irish to emigrate.

The area was always a haven for refugees from oppresion: towards the end of the 19th century an influx of poor Jews from Poland and Russia arrived, some of them used it as a stopover on their way to New York. Today in the East End there are numerous immigrants from Bangladesh and India; if you enjoy curry you can have a feast in Banglatown (D1 52).

The area of the Olympic Park has had a huge makeover for the Games and is destined to open in 2013 as the Queen Elizabeth Olympic Park.

HOUSE MILL / CLOCK MILL   F6 61
Historically known as *Three Mills* and supplying a local Abbey which Henry VIII destroyed, the mills were famous in the 16th century not only for the quality of the flour which was supplied to the City bakers but also for grinding gunpowder. By the 17th century they were producing maize and barley for distillation. Reduced to two mills, the *House Mill* was rebuilt in 1776; the other Mill was rebuilt with a Bell and a Clock in 1817. Through to 1941 they were famous for making an east-end delight or 'mother's ruin'- *Lamplighter Gin*. During WW2 the miller's house was bomb damaged and was rebuilt in 1995 with the original façade and a modern interior. Close by are Three Mills Film Studios making films for TV and cinemas.
House Mill escorted tours Sunday afternoons May to October 13.00-16.00   Charge (children free)
The café opens Mons - Fris 10.00-15.00

THE GEFFRYE MUSEUM   H2 29

Kingsland Road, E2 8EA. An interesting collection of decorative arts and furniture in eleven period settings from 1600 onwards: housed in the original tree-shaded ironmonger's almshouses - fourteen one-storey buildings set around a forecourt, built in 1715 for the old and infirm. It is significant that the museum is situated in an area that at one time was renowned for furniture making.
Tues-Sats 10.00-17.00.   Closed Mondays
Sundays & Bank Holidays 12.00-17.00   Charge

SUTTON HOUSE NATIONAL TRUST   A2 60
2-4 Homerton High Street, Hackney. Unbelievably a Tudor house in the East End that has suvived since 1535. Built by a member of Henry VIII's court, Sir Ralph Sadleir, the atmosphere of past times pervades the oak-panelled rooms in which former occupants, merchants and Huguenot silkweavers, lived at one time.
Open Mons, Tues, Weds 25th July-11th Aug 10.00-16.30
Thurs, Fris 3rd Feb-16th Dec 10.00-16.30
Sats, Suns 5th Feb-18th Dec 12.00-16.30   Charge

THE V&A MUSEUM OF CHILDHOOD   A6 60
Cambridge Heath Road, E2 9PA. Opened in 1872 the Bethnal Green Museum only attained its present purpose in 1973 when the V & A Museum transferred all its child-related exhibits to this subsidiary building. In capacious and light surroundings the permanent exhibits are arranged in three galleries: Moving and Optical toys, Creativity (inspiration - explore - make it happen), Childhood (relating experiences past and present). Distorting mirrors still provide constant amusement for young and old. Adults and children can relate using interactive exhibits.
Five minutes walk from Bethnal Green (Central Line) Tube station. Daily 10.00-17.45. The first Thursday of the month some galleries open until 21.00.   Free

ENTERTAINMENTS

THEATRE ROYAL STRATFORD EAST   **G3 61**
Gerry Raffles Square, E15 1BN   ☎ *020 8985 2424*
Built in 1884, the theatre was extended seven years later
to make it one of the longest of all London stages.
The large stage was used to great advantage when
Joan Littlewood arrived with her Theatre Workshop
Company in 1953. Surviving fires and the bombing
during WW2, the theatre was revitalized on Joan's arrival.

Oh! What a Lovely War was her most famous creation
at the theatre, and was made into a film by Richard
Attenborough. She directed and inspired many other
productions between 1953-79. Art and culture have
flourished since her time with this theatre.

STRATFORD CIRCUS   **G3 61**
Theatre Square, E15 1BX   ☎ *0844 357 2625*
Just a stone-throw from the Olympic Stadium. A
contemporary performing arts venue which features:
music, comedy, dance, jazz, cabaret and children's theatre.
Reached by Central or Jubilee Line tube to Stratford

HACKNEY EMPIRE
291 Mare Street, E8 1EJ   ☎ *020 8534 8381*
This is a beautifully refurbished theatre thanks to the
efforts of Alan Sugar, the billionaire entrepreneur and
star of the TV progamme *The Apprentice*. The listed
building is a former music hall: designed by the
great Frank Matcham, the architect who designed the
London Palladium and the Coliscum. The interior is really
sumptuous; Marie Lloyd, WC Fields, Charlie Chaplin and
Stan Laurel all performed on this stage. Quick rotating
programme changes bring an eclectic mix of comedy,
Shakespeare, jazz, plays, and ballet, and opera from major
touring companies from all over the world to the stage
of this theatre.
*Approached by Central Line tube to Bethnal Green, then
10 minutes by bus 106 or 254.*

VICTORIA PARK

A walk along the streets surrounding
the park proves that this area was
once a very fashionable place to live -
and it still is. Since 1845 it has been
affectionately called the *People's Park,*
and has been the principal open-space
in the East End ever since. Its appeal is
enhanced by being bounded on the west
by the *Regent's Canal* and by the connecting
Hertford Union Canal on the southern edge
where colourful house-boats glide elegantly by.
The central lawn or *Lido Field* was often used
as a place for oratory. Like Speakers Corner in Hyde Park it attracted lively political and religious soap-box speechmakers,
often accompanied by the ever funny hecklers! In more recent years the park has hosted numerous pop-concerts and
has occasionally been the starting point of demonstrations.
Summer or winter the park is a sports place, with large areas for football, rugby, three all-weather cricket pitches, a
three-laned cricket-net where you are free to practise batting strokes and bowling; an athletics track, tennis courts and
a bowling green. The wide pathways are excellent for skating and keep-fit jogging.
Young children also have many delights to enjoy: the pool's playground, a paddling
pool, a deer enclosure, and the model boating lake which hosts an annual regatta
on Easter Sunday. There are several very interesting features to look out for when
you meander through this very underrated - by outsiders - park: the *West Lake*
has a large spouting fountain and on one of the three islands there is a two storied
Chinese *Pagoda* connected by a bridge.

The *Drinking Fountain* has a strangely Moorish look, it was donated by Baroness
Angela Burdett-Coutts, a truly amazing woman of the 19th century - a philanthropist,
the wealthiest woman in England, and well ahead of her time. Charles Dickens
dedicated *Martin Chuzzlewit* to her. Burdett-Coutts dispersed her money not only
at home but to charities world-wide.
On the east side of the park are two alcoves which were originally erected on
the old London Bridge and saved after it was demolished in 1831. By the *Crown
Gates* and the *West Lake* is the *Lakeside Pavilion & Cafeteria* which serves organic
food; also there are a number of good pubs encompassing the park.

DOCKLANDS

(1828) WILTON'S MUSIC HALL	(1820) REGENT'S CANAL	POPLAR	RIVER LEA	CANNING TOWN	BECKTON

(Map of Docklands)

(1820) REGENT'S CANAL
(1828) WILTON'S MUSIC HALL
SAINT KATHARINE'S DOCK
(1881) SHADWELL WAPPING BASIN
PROJECT
PROSPECT OF WHITBY
(1881) LIMEHOUSE
THE GRAPES
MUSEUM IN DOCKLANDS
POPLAR
RIVER LEA
CANNING TOWN
(1806) EAST INDIA
ExCel CENTRE
THE FOX AT CONNAUGHT
BECKTON
(1880) ROYAL ALBERT
WAPPING
CAPTAIN KIDD
(1805) WEST INDIA
M BILLINGSGATE
O2 ARENA
ROYAL VICTORIA
EMIRATES AIR-LINE (CABLE CAR) (1855)
LONDON CITY AIRPORT
TOWN OF RAMSGATE
★ THE ANGEL
Rotherhithe Tunnel
★ MAYFLOWER
THE GUN
CANARY WHARF
★ Blackwall Tunnel ⊖
ISLE OF DOGS
SILVERTOWN
KING GEORGE V (1921)
BERMONDSEY
CANADA WHARF LIBRARY
NORTH GREENWICH ℹ
THAMES
Foot Tunnel
N
CANADA WATER
SURREY DOCKS
DOCKLANDS VISITORS CENTRE
MUDCHUTE PARK & FARM
Thames Flood Barrier
WOOLWICH
MILLWALL (1862) MILLWALL PARK
★ WATERMANS ARMS
ISLAND GARDENS
THE THAMES PATH
DEPTFORD
ROYAL SHIPYARD ESTABLISHED IN 1515
Foot Tunnel
CUTTY SARK
● GREENWICH
FROM ISLAND GARDENS THERE IS AN INCOMPARABLE VIEW OF GREENWICH
FOLLOW THE ACORN SYMBOL
0 Scale of Miles 1 2
0 1 Kilometres 3

★ HISTORIC OR INTERESTING PUBLIC HOUSES

One Canada Square Tower with its pyramid top, fifty storeys, exterior of stainless steel and height of 800 feet dominates Canary Wharf: its red flashing light tells you that this is Docklands. The architect is Cesar Pelli, whose other major achievement was the tragic twin towered World Trade Center in New York. The tower is the apex and the centre of the regeneration area on the Isle of Dogs which now harbours some of the finest modern architecture and planning to be seen in London. The best way to reach the area is by the Docklands Light Railway, which takes you directly to Canary Wharf. At this moment in time it is no Manhattan; it is a daytime, working place, where most of the national newspapers have taken roots (in spite of massive opposition from their work forces). For evening pleasures and other activities you have to go up river, but they are working on it.

THE DOCKS The docks, or the old Port of London used to begin to the east of Tower Bridge, and they stretched down river to North Woolwich. Although their history goes back a long time. It was 1515 when an important phase began; Henry VIII established the Royal Shipyards at Deptford and Woolwich. Wide-spread expansion followed during Queen Elizabeth I's reign, which heralded the rise of London as the world's leading financial centre. The growth of empire, steam-engines and industry of the Victorian era created the need for the new deep water docks, and warehouses which were built to accomodate the huge increase of commerce in the area. The construction site at that time was the biggest ever known. In 1940 Hitler tried to annihilate the docklands. He did not succeed, although he caused great damage: some of the old sugar warehouses burned for many days.

BORN AGAIN The end of the docks came in the 1970's with the advent of new technology: containers, mechanical handling, and roll on/off terminals did away with the majority of dockers. Today, the area is more middle class as city workers move into the renovated iron and brick warehouses. They have their own computer controlled driverless overhead railway, the Docklands Light, and North Greenwich underground station - the largest in Europe - which connects with central London.

DOCKLANDS LIGHT RAILWAY

- TOWER GATEWAY
- BANK
- SHADWELL
- LIMEHOUSE
- WESTFERRY
- WEST INDIA DOCK
- CANARY WHARF
- HERON QUAYS
- SOUTH QUAY
- CROSSHARBOUR
- MUDCHUTE
- ISLAND GARDENS
- CUTTY SARK
- GREENWICH
- DEPTFORD BRIDGE
- ELVERSON ROAD
- LEWISHAM

RIVERSIDE PUBLIC HOUSES

There are quite a few pubs in the docklands area that still retain some of the original atmosphere, and here are a few to whet your whistle.

TOWN OF RAMSGATE
62 Wapping High St. E1. A dimly lit pub where the *Hanging Judge* Jefferies finally got his due. The cellars were dungeons where convicts were kept prior to deportation to Australia.

CAPTAIN KIDD
108 Wapping High St. E1.
Not an old pub, but you would never know. A restaurant and close by a police station.

PROSPECT OF WHITBY
57 Wapping Wall, E1.
The oldest of all the riverside London pubs dating from 1520. Samuel Pepys and Charles Dickens drank here.

THE PROSPECT OF WHITBY

THE GUN, 27 Cold Harbour, E14.
Across from the millennium dome, near the entrance to West India dock, it is alleged to be the place where Nelson brought Lady Hamilton; he lived nearby.

THE MAYFLOWER, 117 Rotherhithe St, SE16.
The Pilgrim Fathers ship was moored here and the ship's captain is buried across the street in St.Mary's.

THE ANGEL, 101 Bermondsey Wall East, SE16.
Parts of this pub are very ancient indeed. It also has very good views up river to Tower Bridge.

O2 ARENA - MILLENNIUM DOME Built to

protect exhibition pavilions from the elements for the year-long show, this massive big top was built to last much longer than the celebrations. Designed by Richard Rogers, it is the same height as Nelson's Column and could encompass thirteen Albert Halls or two Wembley Stadiums, It is now used for concerts,etc.

INDEX TO STREETS

ABBREVIATIONS
The letters following a name indicate the Square and Page Number

App.	- Approach	E.	- East	Lit.	- Little	Sth.	- South
Arc.	- Arcade	Emb.	- Embankment	Lr.	- Lower	Sq.	- Square
Av.	- Avenue	Est.	- Estate	Ms.	- Mews	Sta.	- Station
Bri.	- Bridge	Flds.	- Fields	Mt.	- Mount	St.	- Street
Blds.	- Buildings	Gdns.	- Gardens	Nth.	- North	Ter.	- Terrace
Cir.	- Circus	Gte.	- Gate	Pal.	- Palace	Up.	- Upper
Clo.	- Close	Gt.	- Great	Pde.	- Parade	Vw.	- View
Cotts.	- Cottages	Grn.	- Green	Pk.	- Park	Vs.	- Villas
Ct.	- Court	Gro.	- Grove	Pass.	- Passage	Wk.	- Walk
Cres.	- Crescent	Ho.	- House	Pl.	- Place	W.	- West
Dri.	- Drive	La.	- Lane	Rd.	- Road	Yd.	- Yard

PRINCESS DIANA MEMORIAL FOUNTAIN   B2 40

A

Abbey St.	H4 45
Abbey Orchard St.	D4 42
Abbots La.	H1 45
Abbotsbury Rd.	A2 38
Aberdeen Pl.	A6 24
Aberdour St.	G5 45
Abingdon Rd.	D4 38
Abingdon St.	E4 43
Abingdon Villas	D5 38
Acacia Rd.	B2 24
Acklam Rd.	B2 30
Acton St.	G4 27
Adams Row	G5 33
Adam St.	F5 35
Addington St	G3 43
Addison Cres.	A4 38
Addison Rd.	B4 38
Adelaide Rd.	A4 23
Adeline Pl.	D2 34
Agdon St.	B5 28
Ainger Rd.	A5 46
Aintree St.	A5 23
Aisgill Av.	C2 46
Albany St.	H2 25
Albemarle St	A6 34
Albert Bri.	D4 48
Albert Ct.	A3 40
Albert Emb.	F2 51
Albert Sq.	G6 51
Albert St.	A1 26
Albert Ter.	F1 25
Albert Ter. Mews	A6 23
Albion St. W2	C4 32
Albion St. EC1	B1 36
Aldebert Ter.	F6 51
Aldermanbury	E3 37
Alderney St.	A1 50
Aldersgate St	D1 36
Aldford St.	G6 33
Aldgate	B3 52
Aldgate High St.	C3 52
Aldwych	G4 35
Alexander Pl	C5 40
Alexander St.	E3 31
Alfred Pl.	C1 34
Alie St.	D3 52
Allcroft Rd.	B2 23
Allen St.	D4 38
Allen Edwards Dri.	E6 51
All Saints Rd.	B3 30
All Saints St.	F2 27
Allington St.	A4 42
Allitsen Rd.	B2 24
Allsop Pl.	E6 25
Alma Street	D3 23
Alpha Pl.	D3 48
Amberley Rd.	E1 31
Ambrosden Av.	B5 42
America St.	D1 44
Ampton St.	G4 27
Amwell St.	A4 28
Anderson St.	D1 48
Angel Passage	F5 37
Angel St.	D1 36
Anglers Lane	D3 23
Anhalt Rd.	D5 48
Ann La.	A4 48
Anselm Rd.	C4 46
Appold St.	G1 37
Archel Rd.	B3 46
Argyle Sq.	F4 27
Argyle St.	F4 27
Argyll Rd.	D3 38
Argyll St.	B4 34
Arlington Av. & Sq.	E1 29
Arlington Rd.	A1 26
Arlington St.	B1 42
Arlington Way	B4 28

Artesian Rd.	C4 30
Arthur St.	F5 37
Artillery Lane	C1 52
Artillery Row	C5 42
Arundel Gdns.	B4 30
Arundel St.	H4 35
Ascalon St.	B6 50
Ashbridge St.	C6 24
Ashburn Gdns.	G6 39
Ashburn Pl.	G6 39
Ashburnham Rd.	H5 47
Ashby St.	C4 28
Ashley Pl.	B5 42
Ashmill St.	C1 32
Astell St.	C2 48
Athlone St	C2 23
Atterbury St.	E1 51
Attneave St.	H5 27
Aubrey Rd.	C1 38
Aubrey Walk	C1 38
Augustus St.	A3 26
Austin Friars	F3 37
Austral St.	B5 44
Ave Maria La.	C3 36
Avenue Rd.	C1 24
Avery Row	H4 33
Avonmore Rd.	B6 38
Aybrook St.	F2 33
Aylesbury St.	B6 28
Aylesford St.	C2 50
Ayres St.	E2 45

B

Back Hill	A6 28
Baker St.	F2 33
Balcombe St.	D1 32
Baldwin's Gdns.	H2 35
Balfe St.	F2 27
Balfour St.	E6 45
Bankside	C6 36
Banner St.	E6 29
Barclay Rd.	D6 46
Barford St.	B1 28
Baring St.	F1 29
Bark Pl.	F5 31
Barkston Gdns.	E1 47
Barnby St.	B3 26
Barnsbury Rd.	H2 27
Baron St.	A2 28
Baron's Ct. Rd.	A2 46
Barrow Hill Rd.	B3 24
Bartholomew St.	F5 45
Bartholomew Villas	D3 23
Basil St.	E3 41
Basinghall Av.	E2 37
Basinghall St.	E3 37
Bassett St.	B2 23
Bastwick St.	D5 28
Bateman St.	D4 34
Bateman's Row.	H5 29
Bath St..	E4 29
Bath Ter.	D4 44
Battersea Bri.	B5 48
Battersea Bri Rd.	C6 48
Battersea Ch. Rd.	B6 48
Battersea Pk. Rd.	A6 52
Battle Bri. La.	A6 52
Battle Bri Rd.	E2 27
Bayham St.	A1 26
Baylis Rd.	A3 44
Bayswater Rd.	B5 32
Beak St.	B5 34
Bear Gardens	D6 36
Bear La.	C1 44
Beauchamp Pl.	D4 40
Beaufort Gdns.	D4 40
Beaufort St.	A3 48
Beaumont Av.	B2 46

Beaumont Cres.	B2 46
Beaumont St.	G1 33
Bedale St.	F1 45
Bedford Av.	D2 34
Bedfordbury.	E5 35
Bedford Gdns.	D1 38
Bedford Pl.	E1 35
Bedford Row	G2 35
Bedford Sq.	D2 34
Bedford St.	E5 35
Bedford Way	D6 26
Beech St.	D1 36
Beeston Pl.	H4 41
Belgrave Mews West	F4 41
Belgrave Pl.	G4 41
Belgrave Rd	B1 50
Belgrave Sq.	F4 41
Bell La.	C1 52
Bell St.	C1 32
Bell Yard	H3 35
Belmont St.	B4 23
Belvedere Rd.	G2 43
Bemerton St.	F1 27
Benjamin St.	B1 36
Bentinck St.	G3 33
Berkeley Gdns.	E1 39
Berkeley Sq.	H5 33
Berkeley St.	A6 34
Berkley Road	A5 23
Bermondsey St.	G2 45
Bernard St.	E6 27
Berners Rd.	B1 28
Berners St.	B2 34
Berwick St.	C3 34
Bessborough Gdns.	D2 50
Bessborough Pl.	D2 50
Bessborough St.	C2 50
Bevan St.	E1 29
Bevenden St.	F3 29
Bevis Marks	B2 52
Bickenhall St.	E1 33
Bidborough St.	E4 27
Billiter St.	B3 52
Bina Gdns	G1 47
Birdcage Walk	B3 42
Bishop's Rd.	B6 46
Bishop's Ter	A6 44
Bishop's Bri. Rd	F3 31
Bishopsgate	G3 37
Bishop King's Rd.	A6 38
Blackfriars Bri.	B5 36
Black Friars La.	C4 36
Blackfriars Rd.	B3 44
Black Prince Rd.	G1 51
Blagrove Rd.	A2 30
Blake Gdns.	E6 47
Blandford St.	E2 33
Blenheim Cres.	A4 30
Blomfield Rd.	F1 31
Blomfield St.	G2 37
Blomfield Vs.	G2 31
Bloomfield Ter.	G2 49
Bloom Park Rd.	B6 46
Bloomsbury Pl.	F2 35
Bloomsbury St.	D2 34
Bloomsbury Way	E2 35
Bolingbroke Wk.	B6 48
Bolney St.	F5 51
Bolsover St.	A1 34
Bolton Gdns.	F1 47
Boltons, The	G2 47
Bondway	F3 51
Bonnington Sq.	G3 51
Boot St.	G4 29
Borough Rd.	C4 44
Borough High St.	E3 45
Boscobel St.	B1 32
Boston Pl	D6 24
Boswell St.	F1 35

Botolph La.	G5 37
Bourdon St.	H5 33
Bourne St.	F1 49
Bourne Ter.	E2 31
Bouverie St.	A4 36
Bow St.	F4 35
Bowling Grn. La.	A6 28
Bowling Grn. St.	H3 51
Bowling Grn. Wk.	G4 29
Braham St.	D2 52
Bramber Rd.	B4 46
Bramerton St.	B3 48
Bramham Gdns.	F1 46
Brandon St	E6 45
Bread St.	E4 37
Breams Blds.	A3 36
Brechin Pl.	H1 47
Brecon Rd	A4 46
Bremner Rd.	H4 39
Bressenden Pl.	A4 42
Brewer St.	C5 34
Brick La.	D1 52
Brick St.	G2 41
Bridge St.	E3 43
Bridgefoot	F3 51
Bridgeman St.	B2 24
Bridge Place	A6 42
Bridle La.	C4 34
Bridport Pl.	F1 29
Britannia Pl.	E6 47
Britannia Row	D1 28
Britannia St.	F4 27
Britten St.	C2 48
Britton St.	B1 36
Brixton Rd.	H6 51
Broad Sanctuary	E3 43
Broadley St.	C1 32
Broadmead	A6 30
Broad Walk, The	F1 39
Broadway	C4 42
Broadwick St.	B4 34
Brockham St.	E4 45
Bromfield St.	B1 28
Brompton Rd.	C5 40
Brompton Sq.	C4 40
Brook Dri.	A5 44
Brook St.	G4 33
Brooke St.	A2 36
Brooksville Rd.	B6 46
Brown St.	D3 32
Brownlow St.	G2 35
Brunswick Gdns.	E1 39
Brunswick Pl.	F4 29
Brunswick Sq.	F5 27
Brushfield St.	B1 52
Bruton Pl.	H5 33
Bruton St.	H5 33
Bryanston Pl.	D2 32
Bryanston Sq.	E3 33
Bryanston St.	E4 33
Buck St.	D5 23
Buckingham Gate	A4 42
Buckingham Pal. Rd.	H6 41
Buckland St.	G2 29
Bulstrode St.	G2 33
Bunhill Row	E5 29
Burge St.	F4 45
Burgh St.	C2 28
Burghley Road	D1 23
Burlington Arcade	B6 34
Burlington Gdns.	B5 34
Burnaby St.	G6 47
Burnstall St.	C2 48
Burnthwaite Rd.	C6 46
Burrell St.	C1 44
Burton St.	D5 26
Burwood Pl.	C3 32
Bury Pl.	E2 35
Bury St. SW1	B6 34
Bury St. EC3	H3 37

Name	Ref		Name	Ref		Name	Ref		Name	Ref
Mundy St.	H4 29		Old Park La.	G2 41		Penton Rise	G3 27		Queensbury Pl.	A6 40
Munro Ter.	A5 48		Old Pye St.	D4 42		Penton St.	H2 27		Queen's Club Gdns.	A3 46
Munster Rd.	A6 46		Old Queen St.	D3 42		Pentonville Rd.	G3 27		Queensdale Rd.	A1 38
Munton Rd.	E6 45		Old Sth. Lambeth Rd.	F5 51		Penywern Rd.	E1 47		Queen's Gate	H4 39
Muriel St.	G2 27		Olympia Way	A5 38		Penzance Pl.	A6 30		Queen's Gate Gdns.	G5 39
Murray Grove	E3 29		Ongar Rd.	D3 46		Pepper St.	D2 44		Queen's Gate Pl.	H5 39
Musard Rd.	A3 46		Onslow Gdns.	A1 48		Pepys St.	B4 52		Queen's Gate Ter.	G4 39
Museum St.	E2 35		Onslow Sq.	A1 48		Percival St.	C5 28		Queenstown Rd.	H5 49
Musgrave Rd.	E6 47		Ontario St.	C4 44		Percy Circus	H4 27		Queen St. Pl.	E5 37
Myddleton Sq.	A3 28		Orb St.	F6 45		Percy St.	C2 34		Queensway	F4 31
Myddleton St.	B4 28		Orchard St.	F4 33		Perham Rd.	A3 46		Qn.Victoria St.	C4 36
N			Orde Hall St.	F1 35		Perkins Rents	D4 42		Quick St.	C3 28
Napier Rd.	A5 38		Ordnance Hill	B1 24		Petticoat La.	C2 52		**R**	
Nassau St.	B2 34		Ormonde Gate	E2 49		Petty France	C4 42		Racton Rd.	C4 46
Neal St.	E3 35		Ormonde Ter.	D1 24		Phene St.	C3 48		Radipole St.	B6 46
Neals Yard	E4 35		Orsett St.	G1 51		Philbeach Gdns.	C1 46		Radnor Pl.	B3 32
Needham St.	D4 30		Orsett Ter.	F3 31		Phillimore Gdns.	C3 38		Radnor St.	E5 29
Nelson Sq.	C2 44		Orsman Rd.	H1 29		Phillimore Pl.	D3 38		Radnor Wk	D2 48
Nelson Ter.	C3 28		Osborn St.	D1 52		Phillimore Wk.	D4 38		Raglan St.	D2 23
Netherton Gro.	G4 47		Osnaburgh St.	A6 26		Phillipp St.	G1 29		Railway St.	F2 27
Nevern Pl.	D1 46		Ossington St.	E5 31		Philpot La.	G5 37		Raleigh St.	C1 28
Nevern Sq.	D1 46		Ossulston St.	D3 26		Phipp St.	G6 29		Rampayne St.	C2 50
New St.	B1 52		Oswin St.	C5 44		Pindar St.	G1 37		Randolph Rd.	G1 31
New Bond St.	H4 33		Outer Circle	C3 24		Phoenix Pl.	H5 27		Ranelagh Bri.	F2 31
New Bridge St.	B4 36		Oval Pl.	G5 51		Phoenix Rd.	C3 26		Ranelagh Gro.	G1 49
New Burlington St.	B5 34		Oval Rd.	H1 25		Piccadilly	B2 34		Ranston St.	C1 32
Newburn St.	H2 51		Oval Way	G3 51		Piccadilly Arcade	B6 34		Raphael St.	D3 40
New Cavendish St.	G2 33		Ovington Gdns.	C4 40		Piccadilly Circus	C5 34		Rathbone Pl.	C2 34
New Change	D4 36		Ovington Sq.	D5 40		Pilgrimage St.	F3 45		Rathbone St.	C2 34
Newcomen St.	F2 45		Ovington St.	D5 40		Pimlico Rd.	F1 49		Rawlings St.	D6 40
New Compton St.	D3 34		Oxford Gdns.	A2 30		Pitfield St.	G4 29		Rawstorne St.	B4 28
Newcourt St.	C3 24		Oxford Sq.	C3 32		Pitt Head Ms.	G1 41		Ray St.	A6 28
New Fetter Lane	A3 36		Oxford St.	F4 33		Platt St.	C2 26		Redburn St.	D3 48
Newgate St.	C3 36		**P**			Plender St.	B1 26		Redcliffe Gdns.	F2 47
New Globe Walk	D6 36		Packington Sq.	D1 28		Pocock St.	C3 44		Redcliffe Rd.	G3 47
Newington Butts	C6 34		Packington St.	C1 28		Poland St.	B3 34		Redcliffe Sq.	F3 47
Newington Causeway	D4 44		Paddington St.	F1 33		Polygon Rd.	C3 26		Redcliffe St.	F3 47
New Inn Yard	H5 29		Page St.	D6 42		Pond Pl.	B1 48		Redcross Way	E2 45
New Kent Rd.	D5 44		Page's Walk	H5 45		Ponsonby Pl.	D1 50		Redesdale St.	D3 48
Newman St.	C2 34		Pakenham St.	G5 27		Pont St.	D5 40		Redfield La.	F6 39
New North Rd.	E1 29		Palace Av.	F2 39		Ponton Rd.	D5 50		Redhill St.	A3 26
New Oxford St.	D3 34		Palace Ct.	E5 31		Poole St.	F1 29		Red Lion Sq.	F2 35
Newport Pl.	D4 34		Palace Gate	G3 39		Porchester Gdns.	E4 31		Red Lion St.	G2 35
Newport St.	G6 43		Palace Grn.	F2 39		Porchester Pl.	C3 32		Reedworth St.	A6 44
New Row	E5 35		Palace St.	A4 42		Porchester Rd.	F3 31		Regan Way	H3 29
Newton Rd.	E3 31		Palace Gdns. Ms.	E6 31		Porchester Sq.	F3 31		Regency Pl.	D5 42
Newton St.	F3 35		Palace Gdns. Ter.	E6 31		Porchester Ter.	G5 31		Regency St.	D6 42
New Wharf Rd.	F2 27		Palfrey Pl.	H5 51		Porlock St.	F3 45		Regent's Pk Rd.	A6 23
Nile St.	E4 29		Pall Mall	C1 42		Portland Place	H1 33		Regent St.	F4 27
Nine Elms La.	D4 50		Pall Mall E.	D6 34		Portland Rd.	A5 30		Regent St.	B4 34
Noel Rd.	C2 28		Palmer St.	C4 42		Portman Sq.	F3 33		Regis Road	D2 23
Noel St.	C3 34		Pancras Rd.	D2 26		Portman St.	F4 33		Remnant St.	F3 35
Norfolk Cres.	C3 32		Panton St.	D5 34		Portobello Rd.	B3 30		Renfrew Rd.	B6 44
Norfolk Pl.	B3 32		Paris Garden	B1 44		Portpool La.	H1 35		Rheidol Ter.	D1 28
Norfolk Rd.	B1 24		Park Cres.	H6 25		Portsoken St.	C3 52		Rhyl Street	B3 23
Norfolk Sq.	B3 32		Park Lane	F5 33		Portugal St.	G3 35		Richborne Ter.	G5 51
Norland Sq.	A1 38		Park Rd.	C4 24		Post Office Way	C4 50		Riding House St.	B2 44
Normand Rd.	B3 46		Park St. SE1	D6 36		Potters Fields	B6 52		Riley St.	A4 48
North Row	F4 33		Park St. W1	F4 33		Poultry	E4 37		Rita Rd.	F5 51
Northampton Rd.	A5 28		Park Walk	H3 47		Powis Sq.	C3 30		Ritchie St.	A2 28
Northampton Sq.	C4 28		Parker St.	F3 35		Powis Ter.	C3 30		River St.	A4 28
Nth Audley St.	F4 33		Parkfield St.	B2 28		Praed St.	A3 32		Rivington St.	G5 29
Northdown St.	F3 27		Parkgate Rd.	C6 48		Pratt St.	B1 26		Robert St.	A1 26
North End Cres.	B1 46		Park Pl Villas	H1 31		Pratt Walk	G5 43		Rochester Row	C6 42
North End Rd.	A6 38		Park Sq. E.	H5 25		Prebend St.	D1 28		Rockingham St.	D5 44
Nth. Gower St.	B5 26		Park Sq. W.	G6 25		Prescot St.	D3 52		Rodney Rd.	E6 45
Northington St.	G1 35		Park Village E.	H2 25		Prince Albert Rd.	C2 24		Rodney St.	G2 27
Northport St.	G1 29		Parkville Rd.	B5 46		Princedale Rd.	A1 38		Roger St.	G6 27
Northumberland Av.	E1 43		Parkway	D6 23		Pr. Consort Rd.	A4 40		Roland Gdns.	H2 47
Northumberland Pl.	D3 30		Parliament Sq.	E3 43		Pr. of Wales Drive	G6 49		Romney St.	E5 43
Nth.Wharf Rd.	A2 32		Parliament St.	E3 43		Pr. of Wales Road.	B3 23		Rood La.	A4 52
Norton Folgate	H1 37		Parry St.	E3 51		Prince's Gate	B3 40		Ropemaker St.	F1 37
Nottingham Pl.	F1 33		Pascal St.	D5 50		Prince's Gdns	B4 40		Rosaline Rd.	A5 46
Nottingham St.	F1 33		Passmore St.	F1 49		Prince's Sq.	E4 31		Rosary Gdns.	G1 47
Notting Hill Gate	C6 30		Paternoster Sq.	C3 36		Princes St. EC2	F3 37		Rosaville Rd.	B6 46
Nutford Pl.	D3 32		Patshull Rd.	D3 23		Princes St. W1	A4 34		Rosebery Av.	A5 28
Nuttall St.	H2 29		Paul St.	G6 29		Princess Rd.	B6 23		Rosemoor St.	D6 40
O			Paultons Sq.	B4 48		Princeton St.	G2 35		Rosoman St.	A5 28
Oakden St.	A6 44		Paultons St.	B4 48		Priory Walk	H2 47		Rossmore Rd	C6 24
Oakley Gdns.	C3 48		Pavilion Rd.	E4 41		Procter St.	F2 35		Rothsay St.	G4 45
Oakley Sq.	B2 26		Pearman St.	A3 44		Prothero Rd.	B5 46		Rothwell St.	A5 23
Oakley St.	C3 48		Peel St.	D1 38		Provost Rd.	A4 23		Rotten Row	C2 40
Oakwood Ct.	B4 38		Peerless St.	E4 29		Provost St.	F4 29		Roupell St.	A2 44
Observatory Gdns.	D2 38		Pelham Cres.	B6 40		Pulton Rd.	D6 46		Royal Av.	E2 49
Ogle St.	B2 34		Pelham Pl.	B6 40		Purbrook St.	H4 45		Royal St.	G4 43
Old St.	D5 28		Pelham St.	B6 40		Purcell St.	G2 29		Royal College St.	C1 26
Old Bailey	C3 36		Pellant Rd.	A5 46		Purchese St.	D2 26		Royal Hospital Rd.	E3 49
Old Bond St.	A5 34		Pembridge Cres.	C5 30		**Q**			Royal Mint St.	C4 52
Old Broad St.	G3 37		Pembridge Gdns.	D5 30		Quadrant Grove	A2 23		Royal Opera Arcade	C6 34
Old Brompton Rd.	F2 47		Pembridge Pl.	D4 30		Queen Sq.	F1 35		Rumbold St.	F6 47
Old Burlington St.	A5 34		Pembridge Rd.	D5 30		Queen St. EC4	E5 37		Rupert St.	C4 34
Old Castle St.	C2 52		Pembridge Sq.	D5 30		Queen St. W1	H1 41		Rushton St.	F2 29
Old Cavendish St.	H3 33		Pembridge Vs.	D5 30		Queen's Circus	H6 49		Russell Rd.	A4 38
Old Church St.	B3 48		Pembroke Gdns.	C5 38		Queen's Crescent	A3 23		Russell Sq.	E1 35
Old Compton St.	C4 34		Pembroke Rd.	C6 38		Queen's Gdns.	G4 31		Russell St.	F4 35
Old Jewry	E4 37		Pembroke Sq.	D5 38		Queen's Grove	A1 24		Rutherford St.	D6 42
Old Kent Rd.	H6 45		Pembroke Vs.	D5 38		Queen Anne St.	G2 33		Rutland Gdns. and Gate	C3 40
Old Marylebone Rd	C2 32		Penfold St.	B6 24		Queen Anne's Gate	C3 42		Rylston Road	B4 46
Old Paradise St.	G6 43		Penn St.	F1 29		Queensborough Ter.	G5 31			

HAMPSTEAD AND HIGHGATE INDEX
PAGES 56 - 57

A		Chandos Rd.	G2 61	H		Medway Rd.	C6 60	St. Stephen's Rd.	C5 60
Abbey Lane	F5 61	Chant St.	G4 61	Hall Rd.	G1 61	Meeson St.	C1 60	Selby Rd.	H1 61
Abbey Rd.	H5 61	Chapman Rd.	D3 60	Harley Grove	D6 60	Memorial Av.	H6 61	Sewardstone Rd.	A5 60
Addington Rd.	D6 60	Chatham Pl.	A3 60	Harrowgate Rd.	B3 60	Meynell Cres.	B3 60	Shore Rd.	A4 60
Ainsworth Rd.	A4 60	Chatsworth Rd.	B1 60	Henniker Rd.	G2 61	Meynell Rd.	B3 60	Silkmills Sq.	D2 60
Aldworth Rd.	H4 61	Chelmer Rd.	B1 60	Hepscott Rd.	D3 60	Miflais Rd.	G1 61	Skipworth Rd.	A4 60
Alfred St.	D6 60	Chobham Rd.	G2 61	Hewison St.	D5 60	Millfields Rd.	A1 60	Smeed Rd.	D4 60
Alma St.	G2 61	Church Cres.	B4 60	High Road		Mitre Rd.	H5 61	Speldhurst Rd.	A4 60
Almack Rd	A1 60	Church St.		Leytonstone	H1 61	Montfichet Road	F4 61	Stephens Rd.	H5 61
Angel La.	G3 61	Churchill Wk.	A2 60	High Street	G5 61	Monier Rd.	D4 60	Stroudley Wk.	E6 61
Anthems Way	F3 61	Churchwell Pth.	A2 60	Hitchcock Lane	F3 61	Morning La.	A3 60	Sugar House La.	F6 61
Antill Rd.	C6 60	Clifden Rd.	A1 60	Homerton Grove	B2 60	Morpeth Rd.	A4 60	Sutton Place	A2 60
Approach Rd.	A5 60	Coborn Rd.	C6 60	Homerton Rd.	C2 60	Morpeth St.	A6 60	
Arbery Rd.	C6 60	Cook's Rd.	E5 61	Homerton Row	A2 60	Mortham St.	H5 61	T
Armagh Rd.	D5 60	Corporation St.	H6 61	Homerton		Mostyn Gro.	D5 60	Temple Mills La.	F2 61
Autumn St.	E5 61	Crescent Rd.	H3 61	High Street	A2 60	Moulins Rd.	A4 60	Tennyson Rd.	H4 61
		Crow Rd.	G6 61	Honour Lea Av.	F2 61			Terrace Rd.	A3 60
B		Crownfield Rd.	G1 61	Hubbard St.	H5 61	N		Three Mill La.	F6 61
Bancroft Rd.	B6 60	Cruikshank Rd.	H1 61	Hunt's La.	F6 61	New Plaistow Rd.	H5 61	Tramway Av.	H4 61
Barbers Rd.	E5 61							Tredegar Rd.	D6 60
Barnabas Rd.	B2 60	D		I		O		Tredegar Sq.	C6 60
Beddingfield St.	G2 61	Dace Rd.	D4 60	Iceland Rd.	E5 61	Old Ford Rd.	C5 60	Trego Rd.	D3 60
Belsham St.	A3 60	Darnley Rd.	A3 60	International Way	F3 61	Olympic Pk. Av.	F3 61	Trowbridge St.	D3 60
Benworth St.	D6 60	David St.	G2 61	Isabella Rd.	A2 60	Ordell Rd.	D6 60	Tudor Rd.	A4 60
Berger Rd.	B2 60	Densham Rd.	H4 61			Osborne Rd.	D2 60	
Berkshire Rd.	D3 60	Digby Rd.	B2 60	J				U
Bishop's Way	A5 60	Downsell Rd.	G1 61	Jodrell Rd.	D4 60	P		Urswick Rd.	A2 60
Bisson Rd.	F5 61	Driffield Rd.	C5 60	Jupp Rd.	G4 61	Paragon Pl.	A3 60	
Blaker Rd.	F5 61	Dubenny Rd.	C1 60			Park Av.	H3 61	V
Blenheim Rd.	H1 61	Dunlace Rd.	B1 60	K		Parnell Rd.	D4 60	Valentine Rd.	A3 60
Bonner Rd.	A5 60	Dunmow Rd.	G1 61	Kennard Rd.	G4 61	Penny Brookes St.	F2 61	Vicarage La.	H4 61
Bonner St.	A6 60	Dye House La.	E5 61	Kenton Rd.	B3 60	Pitchford St.	H4 61	Victoria Rd.	H1 61
Borthwick Rd.	H1 61			Kenworthy Rd.	C2 60	Ponsford St.	A2 60	Victoria Park Rd.	B4 60
Bow Rd.	D6 60	E				Powerscroft Rd.	A1 60	
Bow St.	H2 61	Eastway	D2 60	L		Pr. Edward Rd.	D3 60	W
Bradstock Rd.	B3 60	Elliot Clo.	H4 61	Langthorne Rd.	G1 61	Pudding Mill La.	E5 61	Waddington Rd.	G2 61
Bradwell St.	B6 60	Elsdale St.	A3 60	Lauriston Rd.	B4 60			Wallis Rd.	D3 60
Bramshaw Rd.	B3 60			Lee Conserv. Rd.	C2 60	Q		Wansbeck Rd.	D4 60
Brenthouse Rd.	A3 60	F		Leyton Rd.	G2 61	Quartermile La.	E1 61	Wardle St.	B2 60
Bridge Rd.	G4 61	Fairfield Rd.	D5 60	Leyton High Rd.	G1 61			Warton St.	F4 61
Bridgewater Rd.	F5 61	Fann St.	A2 60	Leytonstone Rd.	H2 61	R		Waterden Rd.	E2 61
Broadway	G3 61	Felstead Rd.	D3 60	Leywick St.	H5 61	Ramsay Rd.	H1 61	Water La.	H3 61
Bromley High St.	E6 61	Forest La.	H3 61	Lichfield Rd.	C6 60	Ranelagh Rd.E11	H1 61	Waterloo Gdns.	A5 60
Brookfield Rd.	C3 60	Frampton Pk. Rd.	A3 60	Lwr. Clapton Rd.	A1 60	Ranelagh Rd.E15	H5 61	Well St.	A4 60
Brooksby's Walk	B2 60	Frith Rd.	G1 61			Redwald Rd.	B1 60	Wells St.	H2 61
Bruce Rd.	E6 61			M		Retreat Pl.	A3 60	Westdown Rd.	F1 61
Brydges Rd.	H2 61	G		Mabley St.	C2 60	Rick Roberts Wy.	G5 61	Westfield Av.	F3 41
Burford Rd.	G4 61	Gascoyne Rd.	B3 60	Major Rd.	G2 61	Ridgdale St.	E6 61	West Ham La.	H4 61
		Gay Rd.	G5 61	Malmesbury Rd.	D6 60	Riverside Rd.	G5 61	Wetherell Rd.	B4 60
C		Gibbins Rd.	F4 61	Manbey Gro.	H3 61	Robinson Rd.	A5 60	Wrexham Rd.	E6 61
Cadogan Terrace	C3 60	Glenalm Rd.	A1 60	Mandeville St.	C1 60	Roman Rd.	C5 60	Whalebone La.	H4 61
Calderon Rd.	G1 61	Globe Rd.	A6 60	Manor Rd.	H6 61	Romford Rd.	H3 61	White Post La.	D3 60
Cam Rd.	G4 61	Glyn Rd.	B1 60	Marsh Hill	C2 60	Rothbury Rd.	D3 60	Wick La.	D4 60
Campbell Rd.	E6 61	Gore Rd.	A4 60	Marshgate La.	F5 61	Ruckholt Rd.	E1 61	Wick Rd.	B3 60
Cann Hall Rd.	H1 61	Gt. Eastern Rd.	G3 61	Maryland Pk.	H2 61	Rushmore Rd.	A1 60	Willis Rd.	G5 61
Canning Rd.	H5 61	Greenway	G5 61	Maryland Sq.	H2 61	Russia La.	A5 60	Windmill La.	G3 61
Cardigan Rd.	D5 60	Grove Rd.	B5 60	Maryland St.	G2 61			Wyke Rd.	D4 60
Carpenters Rd.	E3 61	Grove. The	H3 61	Mayola Rd.	A1 60	S		
Cassland Rd.	B3 60	Gunmaker's La.	C5 60	Meadow Clo.	D2 60	St. Augustine Av.	G5 61	
Celebration Av.	F2 61	Gurney Rd.	H2 61	Median Rd.	A1 60	St. Leonard's St.	F6 61	

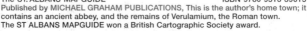

PENGUIN BOOKS
Published by the Penguin Group
Penguin Books Ltd, 80 Strand, London WC2R 0RL, England
Penguin Group (USA) Inc., 375 Hudson Street, New York, New York 10014, USA
Penguin Group (Australia), 707 Collins Street, Melbourne, VIC 3008, Australia
Penguin Books (Canada), 90 Eglinton Avenue, Suite 700, Toronto, Ontario, Canada M4P 2Y3
Penguin Books India Pvt Ltd, 11 Community Centre, Panchsheel Park, New Delhi - 110 017, India
Penguin Books (NZ) Ltd, 67 Apollo Drive, Mairangi Bay, Auckland 1310, New Zealand
Penguin Books (South Africa) (Pty) Ltd, Block D, Rosebank Office Park,
181 Jan Smuts Avenue, Parktown North, Gauteng 2193, South Africa

Eighth Edition Published 2013
2 3 4 5 6 7 8 9 10

Penguin Books Ltd, Registered Offices: 80 Strand, London WC2R 0RL, England